The
Automobile

THE
AUTOMOBILE

A Chronology of Its Antecedents, Development, and Impact

CLAY McSHANE

Greenwood Press
Westport, Connecticut

Library of Congress Cataloging-in-Publication Data

McShane, Clay.
    The automobile : a chronology of its antecedents, development, and
  impact / Clay McShane.
      p. cm.
  Includes bibliographical references and index.
  ISBN 0–313–30308–8 (alk. paper)
    1. Automobiles—United States—History—Chronology.
  2. Automobiles—Social aspects—United States—History—Chronology.
  I. Title.
  TL23.M37   1997
  629.222′0973—DC21   97–12771

British Library Cataloguing in Publication Data is available.

Library of Congress Catalog Card Number: 97–12771
ISBN: 0–313–30308–8

First published in 1997

Greenwood Press, 88 Post Road West, Westport, CT 06881
An imprint of Greenwood Publishing Group, Inc.

Printed in the United States of America

The paper used in this book complies with the
Permanent Paper Standard issued by the National
Information Standards Organization (Z39.48–1984).

10 9 8 7 6 5 4 3 2

For Kevin and Kelly, Susan and Sharon, Molly and Michael

Contents

Tables

Preface

This chronology seeks to list the major events in the history of the automobile. I have sought to be comprehensive. The automobile cannot be understood without knowing something about its pre-history, including such technologies as railroads, carriages, wagons, bicycles and trolley cars. I have included materials on these to the extent that they represented preludes to the modern car culture. This work also includes the materials usually found in automotive histories about the technology, design and production of cars and the companies that make them. The car also demanded a revolution in ancillary fields such as oil production and refining, machine tools and road building. I have covered those topics as well.

The modern automobile is more than just a machine: It created a social revolution. At the simplest level this is geographic—the shape of our metropolitan areas has changed dramatically to incorporate the car. Suburbanization, the evolution of the roadside strip, the emergence of cities without centers and much population migration in the twentieth century are products of the motor car. The car is also a powerful cultural symbol denoting wealth, status and the expression of other social labels. Much of our lives is car-centered. Most Americans sit through two traffic jams daily. At those times the car also acquires an entertainment function. The car is still a major locus for courtship and for family activities. A motor vehicle carries us to our graves.

Finally, the car has generated considerable political activity. Road building has been the most expensive activity pursued by most American states in this century. The car has called forth regulation in other ways, because it has created major new health hazards in the form of accidents and illnesses related to air pollution. The revolutionary land use that accompanied the automobile has required entirely new sorts of land use regulation.

While this work focuses primarily on the United States, it also pays attention to developments elsewhere. The modern auto was a European invention, but technical dominance passed to the United States around 1900. In recent times innovation has occurred more in Europe or East Asia, rather than on this continent. As auto ownership increases in Latin America, Asia, and Africa, it seems to recapitulate the patterns of Europe and North America. Historically, the sources of energy and their management were largely a North American preoccupation. Obviously, this too has changed in recent years.

I have also included in Appendix B a listing of all the automobile museums in the United States, since the best way to understand much of the history of cars is through artifacts.

As with all compilations of this sort, errors and omissions are inevitable, although I hope minimal. Readers who spot any should contact me at the History Department of Northeastern University, Boston, MA 02115, USA, so that they may be corrected in any future editions.

Acknowledgments

This compilation had its origins in course handouts for the class that Gerald Herman and I teach, the History of the Automobile, at Northeastern University. Professor Herman collaborated in its conception and has contributed many items, corrections and bibliographical hints. The work has also benefited from suggestions and faultfinding from students in that course. These include Russell Powers, Martin Sumbung, Katherine Sivak and Brian Cullinane. I would like to acknowledge the assistance of my graduate assistants David Tannenbaum, Mark Szmigel, Margaret Gourley, and Patrick Preston. Brett Abrams did an extraordinary job of tracking down the governmental and industrial sources on which the statistical tables are based. Gary Degon and Jeanne Elizabeth McShane read the manuscript in its entirety and provided many astute comments. Everette Brewer at Northeastern, independent scholar Jane Holtz Kay, and Smithsonian auto maven Roger White all made valuable suggestions.

I did my research for this compilation primarily at Northeastern's Snell Library. Special thanks are owed to Snell's interlibrary loan specialists, Salvatore Genovese and Yves Yacinthe. Other library research was done at Boston Public Library, the Duke University Library, the Library of Congress, Loeb Library at the Harvard University Graduate School of Design, New York Public Library and the Smithsonian Institution. My thanks also to my exceedingly kind hosts on numerous research trips: Kevin and Kelly McShane; Michael McShane; Peter, Dona and Anne McShane; and Peggy and Eileen McShane.

Dennis McNew of the Library of Congress helped with some snags in using the library's American Memory Collection. Anybody concerned with the American past should be familiar with this wonderful collection of over 75,000 downloadable images available at http://lcweb2.loc.gov/am-mem/amhome.html, the library's home page. Russell Koonts helped guide me through the superb J. Walter Thompson Archives at the Duke University Library. Ford Motor Company graciously and promptly consented to the use of advertisements from the Thompson collection. Ford deserves special praise for its openness to historical researchers. General Motors and Chrysler were not helpful at all.

1

Prelude to 1885

c. 8000 B.C.E.

Domestication of animals.

c. 5000 B.C.E.

Sumerians invent the wheel.

c. 2400 B.C.E.

Egyptians build a paved road for sleds from a quarry to the Nile near modern Cairo.

c. 2200 B.C.E.

First suburbs reported, under the wall of Ur in Mesopotamia.

c. 2000 B.C.E.

Babylonians pave their streets and a highway to Memphis, Egypt.

c. 1700 B.C.E.

First chariots.

c. 1000 B.C.E.

In Book 18 of the *Iliad* Homer describes a wheeled, self-propelled tripod built by Hephaestus, blacksmith of the gods.

612 B.C.E.

Biblical book of Nahum celebrates the fall of Nineveh: "The Chariots rage in the streets, they rush to and fro through the broad ways; they gleam like torches, they dart like lightning."

450 B.C.E.

Greek architect Hippodamus lays out the city of Piraeus with a gridiron.

312 B.C.E.

Appius Claudius builds the first paved Roman road, the Appian Way.

170 B.C.E.

Rome paves its streets to ease both travel and drainage.

c. 100 B.C.E.

Following the invention of the camel saddle, the Middle East largely abandons wheeled vehicles for camels.

45 B.C.E.

Julius Caesar bans carts and chariots from Rome during daylight hours to relieve traffic jams.

50

Hero of Alexandria speculates about a steam-powered vehicle.

100

Chinese invent the wheelbarrow.

846

Arab geographer Ibn Khurdadbih publishes the first book of road maps.

c. 900

Western Europe makes great improvements in horse power with the development of horse shoes, the collar harness and the stirrup.

950

Caliph of Cordova, Spain, orders the streets paved and lighted.

1135

King Henry I orders that all British roads should be two chariots wide.

1184

Paris begins to pave its streets.

1209

London Bridge built—360 meters.

1272

Roger Bacon forecasts self-propelled carriages.

1274

British Parliament authorizes the first toll road.

1300

The Strand becomes London's first paved street.

1395

Paris prohibits residents from dumping chamber pots on the street.

1478

Leonardo da Vinci fantasizes about a spring-driven horseless carriage.

1493

Columbus lands Andalusian horses, the first in the Americas.

1525

Public coach services introduced in Milan.

1532

Spanish conquistadors find a 2,400-kilometer paved, tree-lined Inca highway, far longer than any paved way in Europe.

1540

Paris requires horses to walk, not gallop, and bans U-turns.

1553

Queen Mary rides in an imported coach during her coronation.

1555

First enclosed private coaches in London, named after the Hungarian town of Kocsi, where the leather-springed vehicles originated.

1610

First English stagecoach.

During the "starving time," Jamestown residents consume their horses.

1625

First hackney coaches for hire in London, forerunners of the taxicab.

1636

Massachusetts Bay requires its townships to appoint road surveyors.

1645

France issues a patent to Jean Thesson for a four-wheel cycle, which the rider propels by pushing his feet along the ground.

1650

Boston begins to pave streets.

Charles II tries to ban hackneys from London because they are slowing down the carriages of the nobility.

1652

New York City bans galloping.

1656

New York City paves Stone Street.

1661

Spain's Infanta Maria has glass windows placed in her coach, a sign of smoother roads and better suspension.

Philip di Chiesa puts iron springs on a carriage.

1662

Philosopher Blaise Pascal opens a bus service in Paris. Government regulation limits ridership to the bourgeoisie.

1667

In his epic, *Paradise Lost*, John Milton writes about a highway to hell paved "with asphaltic slime."

1673

Post riders take two weeks in the first Boston–New York mail service.

1675

First road link between New York and Philadelphia.

1678

Jean d'Hautefeuille adopts a cylinder and piston to pump water.

1680

Sir Isaac Newton predicts steam-powered vehicles.

1688

Denis Papin builds a primitive steam engine in Kassel, Germany.

1690

Iron rim brakes developed.

1699

Visitor to Boston: "Its streets, like the hearts of the male inhabitants, are paved with pebbles."

1706

Thomas Newcomen develops a steam engine to pump water from mines.

1710

Antoine de la Mothé Cadillac founds Detroit.

1719

Philadelphia paves its sidewalks.

1722

Traffic required to keep to the left on London Bridge, the beginning of the English drive on the left policy.

1736

Saxony requires traffic to keep to the right.

1747

École des Ponts et Chausées, Paris, first highway engineering program, opens.

1750

Horace Walpole complains that London merchants, in imitation of the nobility, are buying country villas in the London environs to be within daily traveling distance of work.

1755

English General Braddock begins first road across the Appalachians from Maryland to Pittsburgh. George Washington surveys the 3.5-meter-wide highway.

1756

First stagecoach service between New York and Philadelphia takes three days.

Ben Franklin produces 150 Conestoga wagons for the British army.

British Parliament requires all traffic to keep to the left.

1761

Philadelphia raises money through a lottery to pave its streets.

1766

John Gwynn, in *London and Westminster Improved*, an important city-planning text, argues for new residential squares in London to allow wealthy merchants to separate home and work.

1768

Boston, the largest city in the colonies, has 22 wheeled vehicles.

Steel springs improve coach efficiency, helping to reduce the London-Manchester trip from 62 to 27 hours.

1769

Nicholas Cugnot builds a steam-powered gun carriage, which he runs into a wall.

Alessandro Volta proves that an electric spark can ignite gases.

C. Varlo places roller bearings on a carriage.

1776

France ends the corvée, forced labor on roads in place of taxes.

1782

James Watt introduces the crank to harness rotary power in England.

1785

Thomas Jefferson writes John Jay about the new French idea of interchangeable parts.

1787

Oliver Evans, an American millwright, builds a continual process, automated flour mill, ancestor of assembly lines.

1789

Daily coach service (6–9 day trip) between Boston and New York.

1791

New York City creates its first one way street. Drivers ignore the regulation.

Pierre L'Enfant introduces the word "avenue" into English in his plan for Washington, D.C.

1792

First U.S. toll roads open in Pennsylvania and Connecticut. The Lancaster-York one requires driving on the right.

French revolutionary parliament requires driving on the right. Napoleon's army will spread the rule elsewhere in Europe. These rules probably only followed existing practice.

1797

In his extremely influential *A Practical View of the Prevailing Religious System of Professed Christians, in the Higher and Middle Classes of This Country, Compared with Real Christianity*, London merchant William Wilberforce argues for separating women from urban life and restricting them to the home. Wilberforce has resigned from his clubs and denounced urban life as immoral and destructive of the family.

1799

Eli Whitney develops the idea of interchangeable parts for muskets.

1800

Wilberforce and 72 other commuters move their families to the London suburb at Clapham Common. Almost all the families are evangelicals.

1801

First steam coach built by Richard Trevithick in England.

1802

U.S. Army Corps of Engineers, which will build roads all over the West, is created.

1803

First coal gas factory illumination (Britain).

1804

New York State requires driving on the right.

English inventor Obadiah Elliot introduces elliptical springs for carriages, the key invention in advancing carriage technology.

1805

George Stephenson constructs the first successful steam locomotive.

Oliver Evans builds the first U.S. self-propelled vehicle, an amphibious steam dredge called the *Orukter Amphibolos*.

Two-wheeled cabriolets, ancestors of modern cabs, imported from Paris to London.

1807

Britain issues a patent for a gas-driven road vehicle.

New Yorker Robert Fulton invents the first practical means of long distance mechanical travel, the steamship.

U.S. government begins construction of the trans-Appalachian National Road.

1808

U.S. Secretary of the Treasury Gallatin calls for national government construction of "artificial" (gravel) roads.

1813

Concord (New Hampshire) coach sets pattern for U.S. stagecoaches.

1814

London requires hackney cabs to carry a number.

1815

First macadam (named after its Scottish engineer, John Macadam) broken stone road—beginning of modern pavement design.

1816

Baron Karl von Drais of Karlsruhe starts a fad with his two-wheeled, walking "hobby horse" or *Draisenne*.

1817

New York Stock Exchange formed, meets in Wall Street under a buttonwood tree. Streets are still often more meeting places than arteries.

1818

London builds the traffic-free Burlington Arcade.

1819

Beginning of English experimentation with mechanical devices needed for road steamers. Rudolph Ackerman invents knuckled steering gear in England, a premature idea. Louis Gompertz devises a primitive rack and pinion steering mechanism. Others devise primitive propeller shafts, universal joints and differential joints. All will be reinvented 70 years later.

1822

President Monroe vetoes a bill calling for tolls on the National Road.

1823

Perhaps the first traffic jam in the United States occurs when too many carriages take the same road in New York City to get to the horse race between Eclipse and Sir Henry on which over $100,000 had been wagered. There is one major chain reaction accident.

Early planned suburban subdivision, Park Village, at Regent's Park, London.

1824

Sadi Carnot, a French engineer, writes *Reflections on the Motive Force of Fire*, a pioneering work in engineering thermodynamics that leads to experiments in internal combustion.

George Kale suggests that steam-driven vehicles will create their own roadways by compressing soil under them.

English inventor Joseph Aspdin develops portland cement, later a vital component of roads.

1827

First American railroads chartered in South Carolina and Maryland.

1830

With the Maysville Road veto, President Andrew Jackson establishes the constitutional doctrine that road-building is a state, not a national, function.

Edwin Budding secures a British patent on the lawn mower, an indispensable adjunct to the new suburban lifestyle.

1831

William Hancock operates a steam omnibus route in London for several months. Eight years later, he will build a lightweight steam phaeton.

1833

First balloon frame building (i.e., using 2" x 4" structural members) built in Chicago—key to cheap suburban housing.

Alexander Jackson Downing publishes *Rural Residences*, establishing the idea of suburban homes with large yards for the American middle class.

1834

American inventor Thomas Davenport builds an experimental electric car.

First inexpensive two-wheeled hansom cab in London.

1835

England ends the corvée.

Duke of Wellington opposes railroads because "they only encourage common people to move around needlessly."

Mary Griffith's urban utopian novel, *Three Hundred Years Hence*, predicts "curious vehicles that moved by some internal machinery."

1837

English developer builds Victoria Park, Manchester, prototype of the planned suburban community.

1839

New York City bans steam vehicles from downtown streets. The city worries about traffic accidents, boiler explosions and coal fumes.

Scottish inventor Kirkpatrick MacMullin builds a direct pedal two-wheel bike with a steerable 30-inch front wheel and a pedaled 40-inch rear wheel.

Baedecker publishes the first European travel guides.

1840

Francis Hill covers 100 miles (169 km) in his English steam coach.

1841

Thomas Cook starts the first travel agency.

1842

An English judge rules in *Winterbottom v. Wright*, a case widely cited in the United States, that coach riders injured in an accident could only sue the coach operator, not its maker.

1844

Friedrich Engels notes that the classes are becoming increasingly segregated in Manchester as the bourgeoisie moves to the suburbs.

Charles Goodyear patents the rubber vulcanization process.

Karl Benz born at Karlsruhe.

1846

Robert Thompson patents the pneumatic tire in Britain, another premature invention.

1849

British scientist James P. Joule formulates the first law of thermodynamics.

1850

Paris begins to lay asphalt pavements. Military engineers urge its adoption, because mobs cannot build barricades with the smooth material.

1852

Richard Dudgeon drives his experimental steam wagon from his Long Island home to his New York office.

1853

Indiana passes the first Dram Shop Act, making tavern keepers responsible for accidents caused by drunken customers.

1854

King Frederick Augustus II of Saxony killed in a coaching accident.

1855

Baron Haussmann completes the Rue di Rivoli, the first of his boulevards that will remake Paris and become a model for similar streets throughout the world. The Parisian bourgeoisie, in part because of government subsidies, choose to live in apartments on these boulevards, rather than Anglo-American style suburbs.

First self-propelled, steam fire engine in United States patented by A. B. Latta.

Yale professor Benjamin Silliman demonstrates that kerosene distilled from petroleum can serve as an illuminant.

1856

Alexander Jackson Davis designs Llewellyn Park, New Jersey, the first suburban subdivision in the United States. Planned in the romantic style with curving, non-gridiron streets.

Isaac Singer begins modern consumer durable industries by selling home sewing machines on an installment plan, first use of that sales device.

Henry Bessemer discovers a process for making inexpensive steel in England.

1857

Frederick Law Olmsted designs New York City's Central Park with the first limited access, grade-separated parkways. Elite carriage owners use the drives to display their status.

British railroads originate automatic signals, with red meaning stop and green meaning go. The colors are borrowed from ships, which are supposed to pass each other on the side with green lanterns. They, in turn had adopted it from a British lighthouse with a red warning light.

1858

Vienna builds its pioneer urban boulevard, the Ringstrasse.

Mechanical stone crushers and steam rollers lessen cost of macadam road construction.

1859

By this date the British physicist Lord Kelvin and German physicist Rudolph Clausius have established the second law of thermodynamics, which Clausius calls "entropy."

Gaston Plante devises the storage battery. Improvements in 1880 allow sufficient storage for vehicles.

Haussmann's Parisian boulevards impress visiting American park planner Frederick Law Olmsted.

E. L. Drake brings in the world's first oil well, in Titusville, Pennsylvania.

1860

Alexander Holley and J. K. Fisher publish "History of Steam on Common Roads in U.S.," which advocates the use of steam autos.

New York City bans speeding by horse-drawn omnibuses.

Traffic count in London shows 57,765 vehicles enter the city daily.

U.S. kerosene exported to St. Petersburg, Russia.

1861

James Hobrecht plans Berlin's boulevards.

First oil gusher in Pennsylvania explodes, killing 19.

First U.S. kerosene exports sent to London.

1863

Jean-Joseph Etienne Lenoir, a Belgian living in Paris, builds a self-propelled internal combustion (i.c.) vehicle and drives it on a nine-kilometer round trip.

1864

Nicholas Otto starts factory to make i.c. engines at Cologne, Germany.

Sheffield, England, chemist H. C. Sorby pioneers in microscopic analysis of steel, a technique that will allow more consistent quality and alloys.

1865

Over 1.2 million horses have died during the Civil War, mostly from disease. Some regiments lost 80 percent of their horses in four years.

Red Flag Law bans road steamers from Britain.

Lenoir replaces coal gas with cleaner burning gasoline and a carburetor.

Samuel Van Syckel builds the first oil pipe line, 9.6 kilometers, Miller's Farm, Pennsylvania.

1867

New York City tries a pedestrian overpass at the corner of Fulton and Broadway, but pedestrians ignore it.

London bans the driving of animals through its streets.

Paris licenses carriage drivers.

Pierre Michaux (Paris) invents the high-wheeled velocipede with turning cranks and sprockets, patented in the United States the following year.

Milan builds the traffic-free Galleria Vittorio Emanuele, prototype of enclosed shopping malls.

1868

Short-lived lighted traffic signal—George and Bridge streets, London.

Joseph Ravel, a French steam auto experimenter, keeps a drunken assistant from falling off his wagon with a primitive seat belt.

U.S. patent issued for the velocipede.

Frederick Law Olmsted plans a romantic-style railroad suburb, Riverside, on an almost treeless prairie outside Chicago. His plans call for curvilinear streets and planting 86,000 trees and shrubs on 1,600 acres. He narrows residential streets to lessen traffic.

1869

J. F. Tretz places a chain drive on a bicycle.

Catherine Beecher's popular *Principles of Domestic Science* recommends kerosene for an illuminant.

1870

Two popular books on gardening emphasize carefully manicured lawns to American suburbanites.

Dr. B. F. Goodrich moves his rubber business from New Jersey to Akron, Ohio.

Liverpool builds a safety island on a busy street.

Italian army issues four bicycles to each regiment.

First rickshaw operates in Tokyo.

John D. Rockefeller forms Standard Oil Company.

1871

William Dean Howells publishes *Suburban Sketches*, a paean to suburban life.

First portland cement works in the United States (Lehigh, Pennsylvania).

English manufacturer begins to sell five-foot-high "penny farthing" bicycles.

1873

By this date, Chicago beef packers have adopted moving dis-assembly lines, forerunners of Henry Ford's assembly line.

Nobel Company (Sweden) develops the Baku oil fields in the Russian Caucasus.

1875

Studebaker, founded in 1854, becomes the largest wagon manufacturer in the world, primarily because it is the first to adopt modern machine tool technology.

Brooklyn omnibus firm introduces a thirty-foot-long, 120-seat horse-pulled vehicle, the largest ever built.

French Academy devises a new word: "automobile."

1876

Engineers pave Pennsylvania Avenue, Washington, D.C., with asphalt.

Nicholas Otto patents the four-stroke i.c. engine in Germany.

Archibald Sharp of London introduces the spoked tension bicycle wheel that makes velocipedes practical.

1877

George Selden sees an Otto i.c. engine and Albert Pope sees his first bike at the Centennial Exposition, Philadelphia. Selden will patent the automobile two years later and Pope will become the world's leading bicycle manufacturer.

Will R. Pitman wins the first bicycle race in the United States, covering a mile in 3 minutes, 57 seconds.

British Parliament gives counties the right to regulate bicycles.

Local bike groups form the British Touring Club.

James Stanley (Coventry, England) places a differential gear on a tricycle.

1878

J. Carhart and A. M. Farrand, driving an Oshkosh steam car, average 9.6 kph, as steam road engines race from Green Bay to Madison, Wisconsin. Shortly after that Wisconsin bans steam road vehicles.

Utopian urban novelist Chauncy Thomas predicts the rebuilding of cities around double decker radial streets, the upper deck of which will be reserved for pleasure vehicles, in *The Crystal Button: Or The Adventures of Paul Prognosis in the Forty-ninth Century.*

Singer sewing machine belatedly adopts the "American System" of interchangeable parts, the only way to meet consumer demand for its product.

Nobel launches the first oil tanker, *Zoroaster.*

1880

Pope's bicycle company is the first American firm to produce ball bearings.

Rhode Island cyclists, recently returned from England, form the League of American Wheelmen, largest bicycling group in the United States.

Average commuting distance in San Francisco: 690 meters for blue collar workers, 920 meters for merchants. Public health officials say that the high population densities due to the limited speed of urban transportation is increasing mortality.

1881

Henry Demarest Lloyd begins the journalistic tradition of oil company bashing in his attack on Rockefeller, "Story of a Great Monopoly," in the *Atlantic Monthly*.

1882

German police arrest Karl Benz for operating a prototype motor vehicle in the street.

Elephant-shaped hotel opens on Coney Island, probably the earliest example of the theriomorphic (animal-shaped) architecture that will become an important element of American roadside strips.

Newly formed Standard Oil Trust controls 90 percent of the U.S. market.

1883

Gottlieb Daimler increases i.c. engine speeds from 100 to 900 rpm by adding hot tube ignition. Lenoir builds the first primitive spark plugs.

Cyclists' Touring Club, formerly the British Touring Club, begins publishing *The Gazette* for bicyclists.

DeDion-Bouton begins to make steam tricycles.

1884

Thomas Stevens rides a high wheeler bike from Oakland to Boston in 104 days.

Courts grant bicyclists access to private turnpikes in New Jersey after a suit by the League of American Wheelmen. The league wins a similar suit over access to Central Park in 1887. These decisions provide the precedents that will stop cities from banning internal combustion cars, as they had steamers in the mid-nineteenth century.

J. K. Starley introduces the chain-driven "safety" bicycle, Coventry, England.

"Record," meaning fastest speed, comes into common usage, a measure of the late-nineteenth-century obsession with speed.

Patent #16027 issued in France for an internal combustion engine to be installed in a Delamaree-Deboutteville steam car.

1885

First survey of urban street traffic in the United States.

Edwin Norton adopts conveyor belts for a can assembly operation.

Benz & Cie., Rheinische Gasmotorenfabrik in Mannheim, Germany, builds the first motorcycle.

Rothschilds enter the Russian oil business.

Royal Dutch discovers oil in Sumatra.

2

From Benz to Ford:
1886–1907

1886

Karl Benz patents the world's first practical i.c. motorcar, after German courts invalidate Otto's patent for the four-stroke engine.

Armand Peugeot begins to manufacture bicycles and builds his first car, a steamer.

Pall Mall Gazette complains of London's "traffic-choked streets."

1887

Ransom Olds constructs a steam car, but abandons research at his neighbors' insistence.

Frank J. Sprague demonstrates a successful trolley car in Richmond, Virginia.

Elihu Thompson perfects electric welding, which allows higher speeds and greater reliability in machine parts.

Daimler operates a motorized taxi in Stuttgart.

1888

Benz cars get their first splash of publicity at a Munich exposition. Berthe Benz keeps the publicity going by driving the family car 100 kilometers from Mannheim to Pforz.

Irish surgeon John B. Dunlop reinvents the pneumatic tire in Dublin, Ireland. After several bike racers test it successfully, it becomes standard equipment two years later.

Piano manufacturer William Steinway buys the U.S. rights to the Daimler i.c. engine.

1889

Schoolmates Andre Citroën (age 11) and Louis Renault (age 12) view five automobiles exhibited at the Paris exposition marking the centennial of the French Revolution.

Leon Serpollet builds the first flash boiler.

Gottlieb Daimler reinvents knuckled (Ackerman) steering gear.

Frank Duryea reads a detailed technical description of a Benz car in *Scientific American*.

First golf course in the United States, St. Andrews in suburban Yonkers, New York.

1890

Organizers of the Chicago World's Fair, to be held in 1893, offer a prize for the best mechanical road vehicle. The offer attracts the interest of inventors Frank and Charles Duryea, Elwood Haynes, Charles King and others.

Henry Leland, later the founder of Cadillac, establishes a machine tool firm in Detroit.

1891

European manufacturers settle on the *Systeme Panhard* (engine in front, rear drive) adopted by the new firm of Panhard et Levassor. Most cars will be built this way until the 1970s.

William Morrison (Des Moines) devises the first functional U.S. electric car, claims 22 kph.

F. W. Lambert builds an i.c. tricycle in Ohio City, Ohio, but loses interest after his prototype catches fire.

Professional rider A. A. Zimmerman does a half mile in 10.75 seconds on his light (70-pound) bicycle.

Michelin brothers begin to put inner tubes in bicycle tires.

William "Plugger" Moran wins the first six-day bicycle race in Madison Square Garden, covering 2,346 kilometers on an indoor track.

First electric advertising sign on Broadway: "Buy Homes on Long Island."

New Jersey is the first state to offer road-building aid to localities, largely because of lobbying from bicyclists.

London shell dealer Marcus Samuels sends the first oceanic tanker, the *Murex*, from the Black Sea to Singapore to export Russian oil for the Rothschilds.

1892

First department store motorized delivery service, Paris.

Sultan of Morocco is the first royal personage to get an auto.

1893

Frank Duryea drives the first U.S.-constructed i.c. horseless carriage, built by his brother Charles.

Inventors show two electric vehicles, a circus steamer and an i.c. Daimler at the Chicago World's Fair. The latter piques Henry Ford's interest. Auto pioneers like the Studebaker brothers, the Duryea brothers, Albert Pope, William Durant, Elwood Haynes, Ransom Olds, and Alexander Winton also went to the fair.

Elwood Haynes's wife throws her husband out of the kitchen after he nearly sets it on fire while experimenting with a gas engine.

Firsts: Wilhelm Maybach (Germany) invents the modern carburetor; DeDion-Bouton introduces shaft drive with universal and differential gears.

Parisian police issue the first registration plates and driver's licenses. They require a driving test.

Panhard et Levassor sell cars to six doctors, four traveling sales agents and three insurance agents.

Rudolph Diesel builds his first engine.

Karl Benz adds electric ignition to his cars.

Bicyclists get Congress to appropriate $10,000 to study rural roads.

Albert Pope opens factories in the U.S. to produce pneumatic tires and steel tubing for bicycles.

1894

New York City carriage builders, J. A. Shepard and Sons, build the largest wagon ever made in the United States. The 7-ton, 32-foot-long vehicle has 9-inch-wide wheels, and requires 7 horses to move it when empty, 50 when full.

Paris newspaper, *Le Petit Journal*, organizes the first motor sports event, the Paris-Rouen Trial.

In England, E. J. Pennington proposes an armored car.

Otto sells his 50,000th "silent" engine.

World crude oil production tops 100 billion barrels, one-half in the United States.

1895

Emile Levassor wins the first automobile road race, organized by the new Automobile Club de France and *Le Petit Journal*, Paris to Bordeaux and back. First racing accident sidelines Andre Prevost's Panhard after a collision with a dog. The Michelin brothers operate the first car with pneumatic tires in the Paris-Bordeaux race. They retire after too many flats.

Center of auto invention is clearly in Europe. Karl Benz creates the first motor bus. Electric taxicabs begin to operate in Paris. DeDion-Bouton doubles engine speeds to 1500 rpm. F. E. Leonert beats a horse in a one-mile race, setting a world record of 1 minute, 35 seconds.

Sewing machine manufacturers Carl and Wilhelm Opel build their first car in Rüsselheim.

Benz places the first i.c. auto advertising in the United States in *The Motocycle*. *Autocar*, the world's longest-running car magazine, first published in England.

Benz's Parisian agent Emile Rogers visits New York City, reports that rough United States pavements will require especially tough vehicles and arranges to have Macy's department store sell his cars.

Frank Duryea wins the *Chicago Times-Herald* race, the first major U.S. auto competition, going from Chicago to Evanston and back. He covers 80 kilometers in 9 hours, burns 3.5 gallons of gas and 19 gallons of water. The race requires a suspension of the Chicago ordinance banning motor vehicles.

New York Times editorial: "The work of extinguishing the horse and placing him in the company of the pterodactyl proceeds as well as can be expected."

Duryea brothers form the first U.S. auto company in September. Benz has already sold 271 cars, Peugeot 170.

Crafty patent lawyer George B. Selden finalizes U.S. patent No. 549,160 for a road engine, which he had applied for in 1877, sensing that it is now commercially practical.

U.S. Patent Office receives 500 applications for auto-related technology.

Pope Bicycle Company pioneers metal pressing techniques, quality control procedures and the systematic, scientific testing of parts.

Standard Oil and Nobel-Rothschild groups form a cartel to divide the European oil market. Prices soar.

1896

Britain repeals the Red Flag Law. Parliamentary laughter greets assertions that the horseless carriage might someday rival the trolley. Frank Duryea wins the London car race held to celebrate repeal.

Benz car traveling at 7 kph runs over Mrs. Bridget Driscoll in London, the first pedestrian killed by a car.

Kent, England, bicycle police officer chases the automobilist Walter Arnold, catching him after eight kilometers and tickets him for exceeding a 2-mph (3.2 kph) speed limit.

First armored car built—England.

Lord Montagu of Beaulieu places a statue of St. Christopher in his car, an early safety precaution.

Fifteen dogs killed in a Paris-Marseilles race.

Americans borrow the French word, "automobile."

William Jennings Bryan campaigns in a Benz while in Decatur, Illinois.

U.S. Post Office begins rural free delivery.

Peak of the U.S. bicycle craze—four million sold. There is even a Broadway show by Kendrick Douglas, *The Bicyclists*.

Residents of the Lower East Side of New York City place glass on pavements to halt speeding bicyclists. Local socialists oppose asphalt paving, fearing that it will attract too much traffic.

Henry Wells hits bicyclist Evylyn Thomas with his new Duryea in New York City, sending her to the hospital.

Lu-mi-num Company of St. Louis produces the first all aluminum bicycle frame.

Henry Ford travels to Macy's in New York City to see a Benz, then builds his first car in Detroit. It disappoints. Charles King operates a successful vehicle on Woodward Avenue. The Detroit police limit him to early morning runs, not to exceed 8 kph.

The Duryeas complete the first car sales in the United States, selling two cars at the Boston Mechanics Fair.

Riker Electric car decisively defeats a Duryea at the first track race in the United States at Narragansett Park, Rhode Island.

Goodrich begins the American production of pneumatic tires for cars.

Daimler begins to market motor trucks.

Benz sells 500 cars, equaling its total previous production.

Cars become the rage for affluent Parisians. One commentator notes: "The automobile is the car of Venus and Cupid." Paris Auto Club offers cars for rent. Paris, with the highest auto registration in the world, is also the site of the first car theft.

Socialist municipal governments in France inaugurate 10-kph speed limits on autos.

A. Borol of Bordeaux opens the first service station.

France equips its army with hinged, folding bicycles.

Henri de Toulouse-Lautrec lithograph, *The Automobilist*—the first depiction of car by a major artist.

Peugeot incorporated.

Baron Henri Rothschild buys Panhard et Levassor (P&L) after Emile Levassor dies in a racing accident. P&L produces the first four-cylinder engine—80 x 120mm. Levassor designed the first steering wheel with slanted column before his death.

Rothschild-controlled Shell Oil Company now holds the Russian oil concession.

1897

Alexander Winton drives a car from Cleveland to New York in 79 hours.

New York City stations police officers at least six feet tall at every intersection on Broadway below Columbus Circle.

Olds Motor Vehicle Company builds its first Oldsmobile.

Novelties: Gilbert Loomis takes out the first auto insurance, pays $7.50 for $1,000 worth of liability, in Westfield, Massachusetts. First gasoline-powered lawn mower—Newbury, New York. First all-day bus excursion—Capetown, South Africa. Gräf & Stift (Austria) offers the first front wheel drive. Friedrich Greiner (Stuttgart, Germany) invents the taxi meter.

Brewer Augustus Busch buys the U.S. rights to the diesel engine.

Stanley twins form a steam car company.

London police fine a taxi driver 20 shillings for drunk driving.

Only six entries show up for a race sponsored by *The Engineer* (London). None finish.

Japan imports some steam cars from the United States, its first motor vehicles.

1898

First independent auto dealership in the United States opens, in New York. It specializes in European imports.

J. W. Packard, irate over a lemon that he has bought from Winton, decides to go into manufacturing.

Firsts: garage (Dr. F. Zabriskie) 2103 Church Avenue, Brooklyn, New York; mail delivery by car (Scotland); tax on cars (France); air-cooled engine (H. H. Franklin); tapered roller bearing (Timken); enclosed car (Louis Renault).

Renault and Goodyear Tire begin manufacturing.

New York's Lower East Side has the highest population densities ever recorded on the planet—757 people per acre.

League of American Wheelmen claims 102,636 members, including Wilbur and Orville Wright.

French graphic artist O'Galop (Marius Rossillion) makes the first drawing of Michelin's corporate symbol, *Bibendum*, a cartoon person shaped like a pile of tires.

Enzo Ferrari born.

London newspapers adopt the railroad term, "car," to describe an automobile.

1899

Winton repeats his Cleveland–New York run in 48 hours. Over one million Americans view the highly publicized run. For most, it is their first sight of an auto.

Society "girls" in Newport, Rhode Island, decorate cars with flowers for a parade, an early example of car customizing.

Novelties: the first American popular song about autos ("Love in an Automobile"); driver's license for a woman (Mrs. John Howell Phillips of Chicago); commercial auto garage (New York City); auto parts business (A. L. Dyke in St. Louis).

Electric Vehicle Company, Wall Street's first adventure into auto manufacturing, makes 2,000 short-lived electric taxicabs.

New York city cabbie Arthur Smith hits H. H. Bliss, the first American pedestrian killed by a car.

Police arrest New York City cabbie James Donahue for driving an electric cab down Fifth Avenue supposedly at 56 kph.

George Morgan, Exeter, England, dies in a motorcycle accident.

Central Park Commissioners (New York City) allow automobiles.

Charles River Speedway, Boston, has the first parkway exit lanes. Gentlemen race their trotters in the high speed lanes.

Scientific American forecasts that the auto will "eliminate a greater part of the nervousness, distraction, and strain of modern metropolitan life."

Ransom E. Olds opens the first U.S. factory built specifically to make cars, located in Tarrytown, New York, close to the huge New York City market.

Value added per manufacturing worker in the United States exceeds $1,000.

Giovanni Agnelli incorporates Fiat in Turin.

French auto workers stage their first strike after a DeDion-Bouton supervisor shoots a worker.

Over 140,000 people show up for an auto exposition at the Tuileries in Paris.

Bullet-shaped, electric-powered *La Jamais Contente* (Never Satisfied), driven by Camille Jenatzy, travels over a mile a minute, 65.8 mph (105.3 kph).

France mandates dual brake systems, decades before most American states.

In England, F. R. Simms attaches a machine gun to a DeDion-Bouton quadricycle.

Hautboy Hotel refuses to serve Lady Harbeton of Surrey, England, because she is wearing knickerbockers while on a bicycling trip. She forces the authorities to indict the innkeeper for "willfully and unlawfully neglecting and refusing to supply a traveler with victuals."

1900

First National Automobile Show held, in Madison Square Garden, New York City.

Short-lived electric omnibus service begins on Fifth Avenue, New York City.

New York City operates the first motorized ambulance in the United States.

Bicycle manufacturer Alfred Pope nearly correctly predicts that U.S. cities will have more cars than horses in 1910.

William McKinley becomes the first U.S. president to ride in an automobile.

Packard adopts the European style, steers its Ohio model with a wheel instead of a tiller.

Gasoline cars beat electric cars for the first time at the Washington Park race track in Chicago.

U.S. engineer Frederick W. Taylor develops high speed steel that allows a tripling of machine tool speeds.

Firestone Tire and Rubber incorporated.

Thomas Edison film short, *Automobile Parade,* and first European auto movie, *How It Feels to Be Run Over.*

Sir John Wolfe Barry estimates that 960,000 suburban commuters enter London daily. Congestion delays cost the owners of the 40,000 horse-operated vehicles in London £880,000 annually. Barry believes that motor cars would relieve this, because they occupy half as much street space as horse-operated vehicles.

Daimler sells a 6-hp car to the Prince of Wales.

French army gets its first motor vehicle, an ambulance.

Michelin offers a free guide to automotive facilities in France to tourists.

France establishes the European pattern, imposes a horsepower tax.

Ferdinand Porsche builds a four wheel drive vehicle for the Austrian firm Lohner.

Gottlieb Daimler dies in Cannstadt.

First offshore oil wells—Caspian Sea.

1901

Daimler Motoren builds a car named after Mercedes Jellinek, the 11-year-old daughter of its agent in France. It is the first production car to break away from carriage design by placing the engine under a hood in front and to have an all steel frame. American car makers will adopt it after its appearance at the 1902 New York Auto Show.

Winton's attempt to cross the United States fails in Nevada.

Curved dash Oldsmobile runabout becomes the first U.S. i.c. car to be made in quantity. The car marks debut of the cheap "gas-buggy" style—low-powered one- or two-cylinder engine, high center of gravity, and open top.

Connecticut is the first state to enact a motor vehicle law.

New York, the first state to license cars, collects $954. Motorists successfully lobby for a liberal 25-mph (40 kph) speed limit.

Mrs. Bernard Baruch's chauffeur runs over a police officer in Central Park, New York City.

David Buick, a bathroom appliance maker, builds his first car.

New technologies: speedometer (in an Oldsmobile); street sweeper (in the United States); production magneto generators in cars.

John and Horace Dodge open a machine shop in Detroit.

Henry Ford drives to victory in his first car race. Board of directors of the Henry Ford Company, unhappy over his concentration on racing, replace Ford with Henry Leland and rename the firm Cadillac.

Wounded President McKinley carried to hospital in an electric ambulance.

Forty buggy whip firms in Westfield, Massachusetts, turn out 20 million horsewhips, 90 percent of the world's supply. All but one will go bankrupt in the next 20 years.

King Leopold of Belgium is the first monarch to drive a car.

DeDion-Bouton sells its 15,000th steam tricycle.

Panhard et Levassor builds the first motor home.

Herbert Austin begins auto production in Birmingham, England.

French cars, led by a Renault averaging 76 kph, take the first 17 places in the Paris-Berlin race.

Spindletop, a gusher, comes in near Beaumont, Texas; the price of crude oil drops to less than five cents a barrel. Two new companies based in the Southwest, Gulf and Texaco, will break into Standard Oil's monopoly. Shell buys Spindletop to enter the U.S. market.

Shell turns down a merger offer from Rockefeller and joins Royal Dutch.

William Knox D'Arcy acquires the Persian oil concession.

Joseph Stalin enjoys his first revolutionary success, leading a strike against the Rothschilds' oil wells in Baku.

1902

Firsts: Broadway show with a car (*Beauty and the Beast*); film with a car used for courtship (*Runaway Match*); tourist buses (New York City); driving and mechanic's school (Boston YMCA); police car (Boston's Stanley Steamer); the American Automobile Association. New technologies include overhead valves (built by Buick engineers Eugene Richard and Walter Marr); the H-slot transmission (Packard); running boards (Northern); porcelain-insulated spark plugs; the Elliot steering knuckle.

Herbert Marble convicted for vehicular manslaughter in Connecticut.

New York Supreme Court rules that only demonstrated "imprudence," not just a violation of speed limits, creates liabilities in civil suits.

Omaha bans autos from its park roads.

Thomas B. Jeffrey Company builds its first Rambler auto, as does Studebaker.

Pierce (Buffalo) builds the first car named after a weapon, the Arrow.

Henry Ford recruits bicycle racer Barney Oldfield to drive his new car in the first races held on the beach at Daytona, Florida.

New York multimillionaire William K. Vanderbilt, Jr., makes the Monte Carlo-Paris run in a record 17 hours in his prize Mercedes, the Red Devil; then defeats Baron Henri Rothschild in a street race in Paris.

Kaiser Wilhelm II, an auto fan after his carriage loses a race to one, offers a prize for the development of an automobile usable by farmers.

Influential German urban planner Herman-Joseph Stubbing recommends narrowing residential streets in new subdivisions to 2.5 meters to restrict traffic.

Leipzig, Germany, transit company places a red/green signal at a street intersection where two of its routes cross.

First eight-cylinder engine: Charron, Girardot, and Voight, Paris.

Dr. F. W. Lancaster, Birmingham, England, builds experimental disc brakes.

English inventor F. R. Simms builds a "Motor War Car" that carries a crew of four, two Maxim machine guns, and a Maxim pom-pom gun.

1903

Ford Motor Company formed, capitalized with $28,000 in cash.

Dr. Horatio Nelson Jackson, heir to the Payne's Celery Tonic fortune, drives his Winton from San Francisco to New York in 63 days to win a bet. A Packard and an Oldsmobile complete the crossing later that summer.

Edith Wharton takes Henry James out for a spin in her Panhard; tells him she is working on another novel so that she can buy a better car.

Boston Rescue League claims that 30 percent of the women that it has saved from lives of sin rode bicycles.

Car makers form the Association of Licensed Auto Manufacturers, a patent trust based on the Selden patent. It refuses to license Ford.

Oldsmobile advertises its cars in the *Ladies' Home Journal*.

Women drivers in New York City form their own auto club.

World's Work, a popular magazine, notes: "Putting a motor car in order is child's play compared with getting a sick horse well."

Novelties: shock absorbers and windshields. Mercedes introduces the gas pedal. Tottenham, England, gets the first i.c. fire engine. Don Albone builds the first gas-powered, three-wheeled tractor, the Ivel; Vauxhall builds the first all-steel-bodied car.

First auto industry forecast that the market saturation point has been reached.

William Phelps Eno publishes the first book on traffic engineering. New York police adopt his rules for traffic and create the first traffic bureau after the *Times* comments: "Only agile pedestrians can survive."

San Francisco merchants build a safety island for passengers waiting for a cable car.

England licenses drivers, including a six year old. No test required.

English motorists claim that a London-Birmingham motorway will ease suburbanization for workers.

French authorities stop the Paris-Madrid race in Bordeaux after ten are killed, including Marcel Renault, leading to a French ban on road races.

1904

U.S. auto production surpasses French.

Frank Lloyd Wright plans a suburban home in Oak Park, Illinois, with a built-in garage.

Carpentry and Builder publishes plans for an "automobile house" (garage).

On opening day for the New York City subway, a diamond stickpin is stolen and 13 drunks arrested.

Detroit bankers force Ransom Olds out of Oldsmobile, preferring a secure luxury market to his vision of a mass market.

Peerless builds the Green Dragon with a huge 1,120-cc. engine, the first American car named after an animal.

Cadillac sends a car up the steps of the U.S. Capitol in a publicity stunt.

Barney Oldfield drives Henry Ford's "999 Monster" at 146.2 kph on frozen Lake St. Clair, Michigan, setting a land speed record that lasts two weeks.

Vanderbilt Cup road race on Long Island draws about 200,000 New Yorkers.

Studebaker sells its first gasoline-powered vehicle.

Locomobile builds an experimental 17,657-cc. four-cylinder engine.

Mack brothers build a Manhattan sight-seeing car.

Harry Weed, Canastota, New York, invents snow chains.

Eleven European firms own plants in the United States, an all-time peak. Fiat contemplates relocating to the United States.

Daimler opens a Mercedes assembly plant in New York City. Within three years all new U.S. cars will imitate the Mercedes design.

Daimler builds a prototype *Panzerwagen* armored car.

Essen bans auto and street traffic from Kettwigerstrasse, a main shopping street.

M. Rigolly drives a Gobron-Brillie to a world record 103.55 mph (165 kph) at Ostend, Belgium—first to exceed 100 mph.

Princess Louise of Belgium elopes in an automobile.

Sir Roger Casement exposes working conditions in the Belgian Congo (Zaire), where Africans work like slaves to meet the global demand for rubber. One Belgian supervisor lopped off the hand of an African who did not produce enough latex.

First six-cylinder engine: Spyker, Amsterdam.

Rolls-Royce begins production.

Ida Tarbell's muckraking best seller, *History of the Standard Oil Company*, starts the journalistic tradition of oil company bashing.

1905

Most popular song in the United States: "Come away with me Lucille, . . . you can go as far as you like with me, in our merry Oldsmobile," by Gus Edwards.

Likely the peak year for rural anti-auto violence in the United States. Urban violence peaked in 1904 in New York City. Stone-throwing mob attacks automobiles on the Lower East Side of New York, one of at least 13 anti-auto incidents in New York City that year.

Half the American motor vehicles are in New York or New Jersey.

New York Auto Show has become the largest industrial exhibit in United States.

Blacks in Nashville form short-lived motor bus company to protest streetcar segregation.

Film, *The Gentlemen Highwaymen*, shows criminals with getaway cars.

U.S. Society of Automotive Engineers (SAE) founded.

Mechanical firsts: tire pressure gauge (Schrader); caterpillar wheels (by Alfred Kilby of Dennysville, Maine, on a horse-drawn wagon); speed bumps (suburban Glencoe, Illinois, which hopes to slow down urban "scorchers"); ignition locks; folding tops; the first double decker bus (Daimler in London); front wheel drive car (Spyker of Holland); patent for supercharger for diesel engines (Dr. Alfred Buchi in Switzerland).

New York City Police Department buys three motorcycles.

C. H. Laessing invents the modern gas station pump.

George Selden builds a prototype conforming to the specifications of his 1877 patent. Its longest run is 400 meters.

Chicago bicycle police officer arrests Flo Ziegfield and Anna Held for violating the 12-mph (19 kph) speed limit.

New York City police set up a one way traffic pattern on Times Square with safety islands in the center.

New York imposes the first one way circular pattern on a rotary at Columbus Circle, based on a concept proposed by the French architect Henard in 1903.

John Jacob Astor, Jr., spends $30,000 maintaining his 20 cars.

American Automobile Association holds the first Glidden Tour to test car reliability and show the need for good roads.

Patrick Tierney of New Rochelle, New York, makes diners modeled after railroad dining cars.

D. Ward King, Maitland, Missouri, invents the King drag that will reduce ruts in rural dirt roads.

Buick spends $100,000 on its racing team.

Mrs. C. C. Fitler wins an auto race before 20,000 spectators in Cape May, New Jersey.

First stolen car in the United States reported—St. Louis.

U.S. engineer Charles Norton's crankshaft grinder reduces a job requiring 5 hours of skilled labor to 15 minutes of unskilled work.

Ford gives workers a $1,000 Christmas bonus. For most, this exceeds their annual salary.

Ford abandons the gas buggy style Model A for the Mercedes style Model B.

Architect Albert Kahn revolutionizes factory design with his "daylight" factory for Packard in Detroit.

William Durant ventures into the auto industry, buying Buick.

Numerous flat tires disrupt the European honeymoon of Franklin and Eleanor Roosevelt.

Britain imposes a gasoline tax informally earmarked for road improvements.

London *Daily Graphic* coins a new word, "smog," to describe the mixture of smoke and fog.

British *Army Service Corps Journal*: "The selection of a car is a grave matter, and similar in more than one way to the selection of a wife."

Revolutionaries set the Baku oil fields aflame.

Glen Pool (oil) discovered in Oklahoma.

1906

Woodrow Wilson, then president of Princeton University, says: "Possession of a motor car is such an ostentatious display of wealth that it will stimulate socialism."

Italian mob assaults William Vanderbilt, Jr., after he runs over a peasant child in Pistoia.

Autos show utility as rescue vehicles after the San Francisco earthquake.

New York makes a few streets one way. Boston follows suit. Urban planner Daniel Burnham recommends banning traffic from some streets in San Francisco.

DeDion-Bouton i.c. vehicles replace horse-drawn buses on Fifth Avenue, New York City.

Chicago developer puts up an apartment building with garage space in it.

New York Herald warns that cars stir up "primitive emotions."

Barney Oldfield says that the hope of seeing someone killed is what really attracts spectators to races on tracks.

Early ad directed at women: "A contented woman is she who operates a Babcock Electric. She knows there is nothing to fear."

Clarence Young (pseudonym of Howard Garis) ushers the automobile into the world of juvenile literature with *The Motor Boys*, first of a 22-volume series.

Ford introduces the Model N, a reversion to the cheap gas buggy type, and produces over 100 per day, as Oldsmobile abandons the gas buggy style, curved dash Olds for a Mercedes style car.

Buick introduces the storage battery as standard equipment.

Front bumpers, built-in trunks and storage batteries become common on American production cars.

British inventor John C. Wood patents triplex shatter-resistant glass.

Rolls introduces the 50-hp, six-cylinder Silver Ghost.

Firestone breaks the rubber industry cartel by signing a contract to make tires for Ford.

Stanley Steamer, designed with the help of a wind tunnel, breaks 200 kph, but blows up while racing, reinforcing public fears of steamers.

Influential city planners meet at the Seventh International Conference of Architects, discuss ways to cope with automobility.

Germany requires vehicles to yield to the vehicle on the right in intersections. After an international convention two years later, it becomes the norm wherever cars keep to the right.

Henard, a Parisian architect, proposes cloverleaf intersections.

Michelin begins to sell detailed road maps to French tourists.

French Banque Automobile begins to finance car purchases.

French trade union leader P. Coupat, complaining that piecework payments, as opposed to hourly wages, hurt quality, warns: "There, automobile snobs, is the secret behind breakdowns on your trips."

First Grand Prix, near LeMans, France, won by Ferenc Szisz, driving 90-hp Renault, averaging 104 kph for 1,232 kilometers. Michelin introduces demountable rims at this race.

France makes Louis Renault a Chevalier of the Legion of Honor.

Farina brothers open their design firm at Turin, Italy.

Grand Prix race driver and bike maker Vincenzo Lancia starts making cars.

Ferdinand Porsche goes to work for Daimler.

Directors force Karl Benz, old and resistant to change, out of Benz.

Armored, but unarmed, military version of the Ivel tractor appears in England.

Napier lists some of its owners in a London ad, including 11 peers, 2 generals, 2 Rothschilds, and a member of the cabinet.

Standard Oil warns that depletion of U.S. oil reserves is imminent.

1907

U.S. car production surpasses all Europe.

Vanderbilt Motor Parkway, a privately owned, limited access toll road, opens on Long Island, New York. It introduces both concrete pavements and banked curves.

Irate at a $5 fare for a 15-block ride, New Yorker Harry Allen introduces 65 Darracq taxicabs into New York City.

John D. Rockefeller switches from a carriage to an automobile.

Secretary of State Elihu Root wants federal troops sent to Glen Echo, Maryland, to block the local marshal from arresting speeding diplomats who have diplomatic immunity.

Atlantic Monthly, Scientific American, and the *New York Times* call for mandatory speed governors on cars.

American Automobile Association and the auto industry lobby unsuccessfully for a federal motor vehicle licensing and registration law, hoping to preempt state legislation. This forces state cooperation.

Newspapers accuse New York City police of fixing traffic tickets.

Firsts: Portsmouth, Virginia, paints an intersection stop line; first U.S. state to require a driving test—Massachusetts; banked race track—Surrey, England; motor truck show in the United States—Chicago; drive-in gas station—St. Louis; car cigar lighter.

Chadwick Company builds a supercharged racer.

Paris-Peking race. Prince Scipione Borghese's winning Itala takes 60 days.

Oakland Motor Car Company (later Pontiac) organized.

Packard and Ford make million dollar profits.

Renault becomes the largest manufacturer in Europe.

Andre Citroën becomes chief engineer at the nearly bankrupt Mors Company and buys it.

As Paris car registrations pass 4,000, Anatole France writes: "The future belongs to the metal beast." French courts rule that horse owners must train their animals not to shy at the sound of a car.

Failure of the first i.c. buses in London leads *The Economist* to forecast "the triumph of the horse."

Tokyo's Jidosha Seisakusho Company builds Japan's first gasoline-fueled car.

Wealthy New Yorkers display their affluence by driving their carriages in Central Park, 1874. Photo from *Harper's Weekly*, courtesy of the Smithsonian Institution/NMAH Transportation.

Phaeton Moto-Cycle

WEIGHT, 220 POUNDS.
SPEED, 10 MILES PER HOUR.
POWER, 2 HORSE.

MOTO-CYCLE MANUFACTURING COMPANY,

J. E. WATKINS, PRESIDENT,
W. H. TRAVIS, SECRETARY,
E. F. SMITH, TREASURER.

1529 Arch Street, Philadelphia, Pa.

Advertisement for an 1880 Phaeton Motocycle, an early steam vehicle, which could not overcome the pattern of urban prohibitions. Photo courtesy of the Smithsonian Institution/NMAH Transportation.

New York millionaire William K. Vanderbilt in his 1901 Mercedes, the first clean break with carriage design. Photo courtesy of the Smithsonian Institution/NMAH Transportation.

A car customized with flowers for a 1901 parade, Detroit. Photo courtesy of the Library of Congress.

Doctor and family in curved dash Olds, an early example of the new baby, new car style of popular photography, 1905. Photo from *Horseless Age*, courtesy of the Smithsonian Institution/NMAH Transportation.

Pierce-Arrow appeals to youth and masculinity. From *Life* magazine, 1910.

In 1912 Waverley Electric becomes the first to advertise in a women's magazine. The driver sat in the rear seat so that she could talk face to face with the passengers in the backward-facing front seat. From *Ladies' Home Journal,* 1912.

Overland advertisement with family and suburban themes. From *Ladies' Home Journal*, 1917.

Henry Ford with his first car and the 10 millionth Model T, 1924. Courtesy of the Library of Congress.

Milwaukee Chamber of Commerce photo with out-of-scale cars pasted on the streets as a symbol of prosperity. From *Milwaukee Illustrated*, 1912.

3

The Model T Era:
1908–1926

1908

First Ford Model T sells for $850. The car marries the high wheels of gas buggies, required by badly rutted American roads, to the heavy body, bigger engine (2898 cc., 24 hp), and convertible top of Mercedes style cars.

Henry Ford writes: "A customer can have a car in any color he likes as long as it is black," since simple styling will keep costs down, his primary goal.

William Durant organizes the General Motors holding company, absorbing Buick, Cadillac, Oakland, and Oldsmobile.

Two hundred and fifty-three other U.S. firms also build cars.

Cadillac wins the Dewar Trophy for parts interchangeability.

Walter Chrysler, then a machinist earning $350 a year, hears the "siren song" of a cream Locomobile with red upholstery at the Chicago Auto Show, and buys it for $4,300.

First family transcontinental trip (in a Packard).

Fifty thousand Times Square spectators cheer the start of the New York-Paris (by way of San Francisco and Siberia) race, won by a Thomas Flyer.

After a bloody seven-week strike, Harry Allen's drivers force him out of the taxicab business in New York City.

Mayor Markwreit of Cincinnati proposes banning women drivers.

Toledo, Ohio, deploys semaphores to direct traffic.

By this date most U.S. states have required mufflers and exhaust gas filters.

First U.S. four wheel drive vehicles—Clintonville, Wisconsin.

First electric lighting system for cars sold—Britain.

Finlay Robertson Porter develops the Mercer Raceabout, prototype two-seater sports car.

British prime minister Herbert Asquith favors a heavy tax on autos, "A luxury which is apt to degenerate into a nuisance."

Kenneth Grahame's novel, *The Wind in the Willows*, parodies the car culture for children.

Edith Wharton writes: "The demands of the motorist are introducing modern plumbing and maple furniture into the uttermost parts of France."

New York State approves $50 million expenditure for highways.

First kilometer of concrete pavement laid on a public highway, Woodward Avenue outside Detroit, at a cost of $13,543.59.

Automobile lovers persuade Georgia to replace the corvée with black convicts in chain gangs. The new system will give the state the best roads in the South within five years.

Over 1,600 delegates from 27 countries attend the First International Roads Conference.

Fiat tries a prototype four-cylinder, 18,146-cc. engine.

Michelin solves the technical problems associated with pneumatic tires on heavy vehicles by doubling tires up.

Bermuda and Nantucket ban automobiles.

Oil discovered in Persia at the site of a Zoroastrian temple.

1909

William Howard Taft rides a White Steamer, the first presidential car, in his inaugural parade.

The American death toll in horse-related accidents is 3,850, more than in motor vehicle accidents.

Sears-Roebuck offers cars in its catalog, and Maxwell begins successful advertising campaign in rural weeklies.

D. W. Griffiths's film *Drive for Life* has a high speed car chase.

Daniel Burnham's famous *Plan of Chicago* contains a proposal for a regional highway network, but barely mentions autos.

Legislators from New York, Massachusetts, Connecticut and New Jersey meet to plan a uniform traffic code.

American Automobile Association organizes first national championship racing series, mostly on roads.

Joan Newton Cuneo beats the famous driver Ralph DaPalma in a road race in New Orleans. Shortly after that, the American Automobile Association bans women from racing.

Maxwell-Briscoe sponsors Alice Huyler Ramsey in the first cross-U.S. trip by a woman driver. Subsequent publicity has a heavy "even a woman can drive" motif.

First event at the Indianapolis Motor Speedway, a hot air balloon race.

First electric horn.

Payne-Aldrich tariff taxes autos imported into the United States at 45 percent.

European countries set common noise and smoke regulations.

Ford opens a Model T assembly plant in Britain.

Paris adopts one way streets.

French playwright Georges Feydeau satirizes nouveau riche auto millionaires in *Le Circuit*.

Italian Futurist Manifesto: "We affirm that the world's beauty has been enriched by a new beauty: The beauty of speed. A racing car whose hood is adorned with great pipes like servants with explosive breath—a roaring car that seems to ride on buckshot is more beautiful than the *Victory of Samothrace*."

Alfa-Romeo, Suzuki Loom Works and Hudson Motor Car Company founded.

Anglo-Persian Oil Company (later British Petroleum) formed.

1910

Saturday Evening Post coins the expression "traffic jam."

Rev. I. T. Lansing of Scranton, Pennsylvania, complains that Americans spend more money on cars than "church work." Chancellor James Day of Syracuse University complains that young men are putting off marriage so that they can buy cars.

Victor Appleton, Jr. (pseudonym for Edward Stratemeyer), publishes *Tom Swift and His Electric Runabout, or the Speediest Car on the Road*. Tom will not admit women to his workshop, enjoys running over chickens and dogs.

Laura Dent Crane publishes *The Automobile Girls along the Hudson*, first of the six-volume Automobile Girls Series.

Barney Oldfield beats the black heavyweight champion Jack Johnson in a match race. A *New York Sun* headline reads, "Oldfield Saves White Race." AAA bans blacks from racing as "detrimental to the sport."

Durant loses control of General Motors (G.M.) to New York bankers after its near bankruptcy.

Failure rate in the U.S. auto industry to date—75 percent.

Torpedo bodies (dashboard closer to driver, high sides) introduced.

Left side drive becomes the standard for U.S. cars.

Austria begins the European pattern of symbolic (not word) signs with a brake sign for steep hills.

First V-8 engine: Model CL DeDion-Bouton.

Isotta Fraschini pioneers four-wheel disc brakes.

Neon advertising signs appear for the first time—Paris Automobile Show.

Otto Julius Bierbaum publishes the first German book on auto touring.

Germany licenses drivers.

Friedrich Berjius, a German chemist, discovers the hydrogenation process to convert coal into gasoline, a process that will later allow war transport in petroleum-short Germany.

Rising rubber prices trigger the development of European-owned plantations in Southeast Asia.

Mexican oil found ("Golden Lane").

1911

U.S. Circuit Court rules the Selden patent "valid but not infringed," ending its disruption of the auto industry.

Most U.S. car makers offer demountable rims as standard equipment, enormously easing tire changes.

U.S. farmers own 85,000 automobiles.

Durant reenters the auto business, buying the Chevrolet Motor Company.

New York Stock Exchange lists auto stocks for the first time.

Studebaker begins to offer customers credit.

Chicago imposes a short-lived 30-minute parking limit in the Loop.

Thirty car dealers are already in business on Van Ness Avenue, San Francisco.

Frederick W. Taylor publishes *Principles of Scientific Management*, a path-breaking treatise on factory administration.

Ray Harroun wins the first Indianapolis 800 (500 miles) in a Marmon Wasp with the first rearview mirror.

Model T Fords win 12 major U.S. races, including one over the world-record-holding Blitzen Benz.

Trenton, Michigan (near Detroit), paints the first highway center line, part of Wayne County's program for placing them on curves and bridges.

New York is first state to limit highway billboards.

Britain enacts its first horsepower tax, guaranteeing that British automotive design will be backward.

Rolls-Royce adopts its famous *Spirit of Ecstasy* hood ornament.

Aimée-Jules Dalou's memorial sculpture of Emile Levassor at the wheel of a car is unveiled in Paris.

France switches to driving on the left and abolishes the speed limit. Road deaths soar.

First running of the Monte Carlo Rally—Turcat Mery wins.

Italian army adopts the first armored cars (and airplanes) in combat, Italo-Turkish War in Libya.

U.S. Supreme Court breaks up Standard Oil in an antitrust action. Three major oil companies will result: Exxon (née Esso), Mobil (formerly Standard Oil of New York), and Socal (formerly Standard Oil of California).

Gasoline sales surpass kerosene sales in the United States.

1912

For the first time, New York, London and Paris manifest more motor vehicle than horse-drawn traffic and suffer more fatalities caused by cars than wagons.

New Yorkers brag that Fifth Avenue has more motor traffic than any other street in the world. The city now stations traffic police at every corner south of 42nd Street.

New York State has piled up $100 million in highway debt, more than all other states together.

Bronx River Parkway Commission hires Jay Downer as its chief engineer and Gilmore Clark as its landscape architect. They will design the first urban parkway planned for motor vehicles.

Golden Gate Park, San Francisco, opens its park drives to cars, the last urban park in the United States to do so.

Theodore Roosevelt injured in an auto accident while campaigning for president.

Motor Car magazine writes about motor campers: "Thoreau at 29 cents a gallon." "Time and space are at your beck and call; your freedom is complete."

Boston architect Harry Morton Ramsey: "The garage should not convey too strongly at first sight the idea of garage."

Hal Roach presents the first of the Keystone Kops film series, which feature nihilistic car chases.

Safety expert Edward Cornell: "Any nerve specialist will tell you that auto riding has a sad effect on motherhood."

Waverly Electric advertises a car with a rear-facing front seat and steering lever for drivers in the center of the back seat. The arrangement allows drivers to converse face to face with all passengers.

First self-starter and independent electrical system on a production car, a Cadillac built by Henry Leland and Charles F. Kettering.

Society of Automotive Engineers standardizes screw threads and other car parts.

Novelties: pressed steel body developed by Edward Gowen Budd; carbon black as a tire strengthener; dump truck and bookmobile (Washington County, Maryland).

Pierce Arrow makes a 13,678-cc. engine.

Competitors get the Indianapolis Speedway to ban Model Ts, ostensibly because they are too light.

Ford has 7,000 dealerships in the United States, at least one in every town with a population over 2,000.

Walter Chrysler takes a 50 percent pay cut to become a plant manager for Buick.

Henry Ford breaks a strike at a Buffalo plant by closing it and shipping its machinery to Detroit.

Packard truck makes a coast-to-coast trip.

German, British and French manufacturers demand protection from U.S. exports.

Henry Ford sends Charles Sorenson to Britain, where he breaks the Metal Workers Union in the Model T plant.

Kaiser Wilhelm owns 25 cars; Czar Nicholas II has 21. Emperor Mutsuhito of Japan orders 2 Mercedes cars.

Louis Renault visits Taylor and Ford in the United States. His attempts to "Taylorize" his factory leads to a major strike.

Writer Marcel Proust has lined his study with cork to limit traffic noise.

Paris adopts New York's Eno system of traffic regulation, and its police plan to shoot out the tires of cars whose drivers refuse orders to stop.

Norway requires auto insurance for all drivers.

Renault sells 100 taxicabs in Mexico City.

First offshore oil wells (Southern California).

Britain decides to switch its naval fuel from coal to oil and starts to buy a majority share of British Petroleum.

1913

Clarence W. Avery installs the first moving production line at Ford's Highland Park plant. Within two years it will cut assembly time per car from 12 hours to 93 minutes.

More cars than wagons and carriages produced in the United States.

Ford factories have a 370 percent labor turnover and a 10 percent daily absentee rate. Seventy-one percent of new employees last less than 5 days.

Ford creates a centralized employment office, diminishing the foremen's authority.

Ford Motor Company ends outside lunch breaks after 3,000 workers attend union rally by the Industrial Workers of the World, a syndicalist union.

Ford abandons racing because it has become too specialized to bear any relation to production cars and fatalities generate bad publicity.

Andre Citroën and Giovanni Agnelli (Fiat head) visit Ford's factories.

Clarke, Leslie and Abraham's song, "He'll Have to Get Under, Get Out & Get Under," becomes a big hit.

New York State outlaws drunken driving. New York City paints pedestrian crossing lines on the corner of 5th Avenue and 42nd Street. Newark bans parking on some downtown side streets.

Baltimore motorizes garbage collection.

President Wilson's car hits a messenger boy. Wilson and his chauffeur accompany the boy to the emergency room of a nearby hospital, where Wilson promises him a new bike.

Phoenix, Arizona, newspaper, *Arizona Republican*, coins a new word: "motorcade."

U.S. Congress authorizes Rock Creek Parkway, Washington, D.C., completed in 1935.

Innovations: automotive hearse—Chicago; roadside motor court—Douglas, Arizona; automatic drive for starters marketed—Bendix; forced-feed lubrication and worm bevel gears—Packard; radial tire patented—England.

New U.S. income tax exempts property tax and interest charges for mortgage holders, a subsidy to suburbanization.

U.S. Post Office begins parcel post delivery.

Alabama is the last government in the Western world to abandon the corvée.

Frederick Law Olmsted, Jr., plans the elite Palos Verdes subdivision in Los Angeles on the model of his father's Riverside, Illinois, plan.

Paris Omnibus Comany gives up its last horse.

British Morris begins to import American parts, becomes the first European firm to produce one car per worker per year.

English Parliament requires horse-drawn vehicles to yield the right of way to cars.

Daimler shuts down its U.S. factory.

Austrian Daimler fires Ferdinand Porsche for throwing a spark plug at another director during a board meeting. He goes to Daimler-Benz.

Standard Oil introduces the Buron cracking process, doubling fuel production.

1914

Harvard president Eliot writes in the *National Geographic*: "The evils which attend the growth of modern cities and the factory system are too great for the human body to endure without the consolation of natural scenery."

"Jitney" craze leads to the first daily rush hour, auto traffic jams and a surge in accidents in U.S. cities.

Ad in the *New York Times*: "Straphangers! Attention! The Saxon sets you free."

Chevrolet introduces its "bow tie" logo.

Work begun on the Lincoln Highway, the first transcontinental road, from New York to San Francisco.

Kentucky claims 16,000 kilometers of macadam (gravel) roads completed in previous two years.

Detroit police sergeant Harry Jackson builds the first stop sign, financed by the Auto Club of Michigan. The city also begins to tow away cars parked in crosswalks.

Cleveland installs the first permanent traffic lights (red signal only) at the corner of Euclid Avenue and 105th Street.

New York begins to coordinate the flow of traffic on 5th Avenue, with semaphores and police officers in towers at each corner.

New York City requires horse-drawn vehicles to have headlights and taillights at night.

Detroit passes a law forbidding gas pumps at curbs.

Newark bans left turns at the corner of Broad Street and Market Street.

Fundamentalist Dunkard sect sanctions driving Model Ts, but not Buicks. One elder complains that car riding both exalted and corrupted his heart.

Louisiana is the last state to require car registration.

Novelties: traffic-activated semaphore at a railroad crossing—California; adjustable seats; mass-produced V-8 engine—Cadillac; spiral bevel gear—Packard; headlights built into the car body—Pierce.

Henry Ford raises minimum daily wage from $2.30 to $5.

Ford fires 900 Greek and Russian Orthodox workers for skipping work on the Julian calendar Christmas. Less than 30 percent of Ford workers are U.S. born.

Clara Ford (wife of Henry) buys herself a Detroit Electric.

First Dodge comes off the assembly line.

About 195 American firms make faddish cyclecars, a lightweight meld of bicycle and car with very small engines, bicycle wheels and plywood bodies.

National Auto Chamber of Commerce, a trade association, founded.

Mercedes briefly offers a primitive automatic transmission.

Serbian nationalists assassinate Archduke Ferdinand of Austria in Sarajevo while he is riding in an open touring car made by Gräf & Stift (the Rolls-Royce of Austria).

World War I breaks out. The French army has 265 motor vehicles; the British army, 0.

Renault taxis (driven by, among others, Gertrude Stein and Jean Cocteau) save Paris by rushing troops to the front before the first Battle of the Marne.

Germans capture and pillage the Panhard et Levassor factory.

Daimler applies Ford-style serial production for the first time to make aircraft engines for the German war effort, begins to hire women workers for the first time.

British War Office begins to think about armored, tracked vehicles that can overcome machine guns and barbed wire.

Kwaishinsha Company makes the first Dat car ("sun" added to name in 1931).

Shell buys the Rothschilds' Russian interests.

1915

Los Angeles annexes the San Fernando Valley.

Detroit converts Cadillac Square into a 400-vehicle parking lot. At about this time, Cincinnati turns down proposals to level Fountain Square for parking and New York, the Fifty-ninth Street Plaza.

Daily traffic at the corner of Fifth Avenue and 34th Street: 25,580 vehicles; 142,230 pedestrians.

Queens, New York City, suburban developers are widening the traditional house lot to allow room for residents to park autos.

Industrialists and casualty insurers form the National Safety Council.

U.S. Post Office threatens to deny rural free delivery to communities with poor roads.

Emily Post motors coast to coast in a widely publicized stunt. Her son drives every kilometer of the way.

C. D. Noonan of Paris, Illinois, advertises a kit to add overhead valves to Fords for street racing.

Ford spends $100,000 on social investigators to ensure that his workers deserve $5 a day by attending church, staying sober, and having otherwise acceptable lifestyles.

Henry Ford opposes war preparedness.

Assembly line at Ford's San Francisco branch factory becomes a major attraction at the Pan Pacific Exposition, San Diego.

Shell operates a shell-shaped station at the Exposition.

With Dupont family aid, Durant and Chevrolet recapture G.M. Chevrolet introduces the popular 490 model, which will sell 100,000 units within two years.

Frank Duryea liquidates his car firm, goes into retirement at age 38.

U.S. auto industry agrees to cross-license patents.

General Tire incorporated.

Cadillac offers tilt beam headlamps.

Detroit blacksmith August Fruehaf builds the first tractor trailer.

French modernist painter Francis Picabia, visiting the United States, writes: "The machine has become more than just an adjunct of human life. It is really part of human life—perhaps the very soul." His famous painting, *Portrait of a Young American Woman in the State of Nudity*, depicts a spark plug.

First military tests of tanks (developed as "land ships" by the British Royal Navy).

1916

First complaints surface about New York City's parking problems.

D. W. Griffiths's famous film, *Intolerance*, has an extended car chase scene.

Walter Murphy begins a Hollywood tradition, customizing cars for the stars.

Clarence Saunders opens the first self-service food market—Piggly-Wiggly (Memphis, Tennessee).

Arthur Trachte (Madison, Wisconsin) builds the first prefabricated steel garage.

President Woodrow Wilson signs the Federal Aid Road Act, which provides the first federal money for road building.

Wilson turns down the offer of a free Cadillac, preferring a Pierce-Arrow.

Packard offers the first production 12-cylinder cars.

Victims of New York City car accidents who have been injured by property-less, uninsured drivers organize to demand compulsory insurance.

Auto lover James Doolittle: "The solution [to accidents] is to repeal the speed laws and call reckless drivers before the Blindfold Goddess, Justice, standing on the Common Law."

New York State Court of Appeals settles a major legal issue: manufacturers, not dealers, are responsible for defective products.

American Automobile Association (AAA) sanctions road races for the last time. Manufacturers prefer track races, which are safer, more profitable, and eliminate European competitors.

U.S. Army supplies General Pershing's Punitive Expedition in Mexico by truck.

Stutz Bearcat breaks the record, going from San Diego to New York in 11 days, 7 1/2 hours.

Studebaker offers a one-of-a-kind, gold plated car for $35,000 at the New York Auto Show.

First mobile cement mixer truck.

Slanted windshields and door locks become common and hand-operated windshield wipers are introduced.

As interest in electric cars wanes, Woods tries to salvage the technology with a dual-engined (gas and electric) car.

Goodyear becomes the leading tire producer.

Charles W. Nash, General Motors' president, leaves to take over the Thomas B. Jeffrey Company, now renamed Nash.

Ford's English language school graduates 16,000 immigrant employees.

Henry Ford: "History is more or less bunk."

Packard, with a majority of immigrant employees, announces that it will only promote U.S. citizens.

National Auto Chamber of Commerce claims that installment purchase plans are unethical.

Ford expands into the third world, opening a plant in Buenos Aires.

Tokyo Ishikawajima Shipbuilding, later Isuzu, builds its first car.

France supplies the besieged fortress of Verdun solely by motor vehicles, mostly Berliet trucks.

Britain deploys tanks at the Battle of the Somme.

1917

United States enters World War I. The transition to war production is sluggish, although the 128,000 trucks produced in 1917 are five times the 1914 level. The first U.S. Army truck convoy takes three weeks to go from Toledo to Baltimore, averaging 23 kph.

U.S. auto industry buys 25 percent of the advertising space in nationally circulated magazines.

Auto advertising guru Ned Jordan claims: "While men buy cars, women choose them."

Woodrow Wilson is the last president to use a horse and carriage in his inaugural parade.

Seat belts tried in airplanes.

First electric windshield wiper.

Barney Oldfield builds an aluminum safety racer with a roll bar, streamlining, and screen-covered slots for windows.

Aviation pioneer Glenn Curtiss builds an experimental flying car.

Albert Kahn designs Ford's River Rouge plant, the largest industrial complex on earth.

Leland brothers (founders of Cadillac) resign from G.M. to form Lincoln, citing Durant's initial refusal to participate in war production.

Dupont buys a 23 percent share of G.M.

Chevrolet begins to offer closed cars, a sign that consumers want to drive cars year round.

Paige introduces the rumble seat.

Ford begins tractor production.

Proportion of supervisors and clerks in Ford factories is triple the 1914 level.

Bostonians coin a new word: "jaywalker."

Women hold 8 percent of the driver's licenses in Massachusetts, are involved in only 4 percent of the accidents. In the Los Angeles area, 23 percent of drivers are women, the highest rate in the United States.

Last urban stampede: 500 horses run amok in downtown Columbia, Tennessee.

National Conference on City Planning hears calls for a new profession: traffic engineers.

Atlanta plans a 51-meter-wide parkway to serve as a ghetto wall between black and white neighborhoods.

Chicago judge Joseph Sabath presides over the first traffic court. Chicago police now issue tickets, rather than arresting motorists.

Canada builds the St. Lawrence, Quebec, Bridge, the longest vehicular bridge in the world—549 meters.

Henri Matisse paints *Route de Villacoubay*, an impressionist view from a car.

Novelist Gertrude Stein takes a mechanics course to become a volunteer ambulance driver for the French army. Ernest Hemingway follows suit in Italy.

Michelin begins to plan postwar guides to the battlefields in France with French, English, and German editions.

British launch an offensive with massed tanks at Cambrai.

Lenin commandeers the czar's Rolls-Royce.

Mitsubishi Shipbuilding builds its Model A, a luxury car.

Balfour Declaration: Britain guarantees a Jewish homeland in the Middle East.

World oil production tops 500 billion barrels, 60 percent in the United States.

Mexico is the first third world country to nationalize some U.S. oil holdings.

U-boat offensive reduces Britain to two months' oil supply.

British sappers sabotage the Rumanian oil fields, cutting off German supplies for six months.

1918

Major oil shortages plague the German economy, contributing to home front unrest.

Germany deploys tanks for the first time: too little, too late.

Daimler's work force (40% women) completes its 20,000th aircraft engine. Its wartime profits (up 35%) become a major scandal.

New York Times objects to wartime regulations classifying all cars as pleasure vehicles, thus allowing the cutoff of steel supplies to the auto industry.

Three months before the armistice, the U.S. auto industry finally agrees to restrict passenger car construction. Ford's war effort is especially bad.

U.S. rail system fails under wartime stress. U.S. Army orders 17,000 trucks driven from the Midwest to New York. The resulting traffic tears up roads badly. The government introduces the Liberty truck (prototype of modern trucks). Total U.S. wartime truck production: 355,000.

New York City adopts red and green traffic lights. They are manually operated by police officers.

Leading cause of death for Cincinnati children—auto accidents.

St. Louis places eight spotlights on buildings to illuminate traffic officers at night and on rainy days.

G.M. buys Fisher Body, a custom coach builder.

U.S. car makers offer carburetors that allow kerosene as a fuel.

Freelan Stanley killed in a car crash.

Cannonball Baker visits all 48 state capitols in 83 days in a Revere.

Ignition locks become standard on new U.S. cars, a sign that car theft has become commonplace.

Wisconsin numbers its highways.

In Connecticut property losses attributable to auto accidents exceed those attributable to forest fires for the first time.

World War I ends. The French army has 265,000 motor vehicles.

Britain knights the president of Ford-England for producing 50,000 vehicles during World War I.

Fiat has produced more wartime trucks than any other producer: 45,000.

Booth Tarkington's best-selling novel, *The Magnificent Ambersons*, depicts automobile industry millionaires.

Carl Sandburg's poem, "Portrait of a Motorcar," notes the sexual attraction and conquest of nature themes in automobility.

Henry Ford, who refuses to accept donations or campaign, loses the election for U.S. senator from Michigan by 4,334 votes. The U.S. Senate later refuses to seat his rival because of electoral fraud.

Detroit elects Ford's associate, James Couzens, as mayor.

Mt. Royal (Montreal)—world's longest vehicular tunnel—5.1 kilometers.

Fiat turns down a job application from a promising young engineer, Enzo Ferrari, who goes to Alfa-Romeo instead.

American engineer William Gorham arrives in Japan, builds a mechanized rickshaw.

1919

G.M. extends credit to customers (GMAC).

Henry Ford buys out his investors and becomes sole owner of Ford Motor Company.

Clarence Avery introduces continuous process plate glass at Ford, making cheap closed cars possible.

Ford tests ergonomics with a human dummy.

Ford begins to plan Greenfield Village, a museum devoted to rural life and the history of technology.

Ford employs over 9,000 disabled workers, far more than any other firm.

Ned Jordan plugs his Playboy car: "It's a car for a man's man . . . or a girl who loves the out-of-doors."

Young U.S. Army captain Dwight Eisenhower leads a coast-to-coast convoy, which averages less than 9 kph (6 mph).

Oregon imposes the first state gasoline tax (1¢ per gallon).

New York State's Knight-Wheelock Bill mandates driving tests for new licenses, a traffic court and revocation of licenses for some offenses.

National Association of Taxicab Owners (NATO) founded.

Tampa turns DeSoto Park into the first motor camping ground in the South.

René Thomas becomes the first driver to break 100 mph (160 kph) at the Indianapolis 800.

American Express issues the first traveler's checks.

Hispano-Suiza introduces an aircraft-engine-derived overhead cam engine that will set the pattern for sports cars in the 1920s. It also makes the first power brakes.

Isotta-Fraschini makes the first production straight-8 engines.

Soviet industrial planners tour United States, meet Henry Ford.

Andre Citroën uses his wartime profits from making artillery shells to start his car company and introduces the Ford-style assembly line to Europe.

Eccles Transport kicks off the regular manufacture of caravans (mobile homes) in England.

German police kill 17 striking auto workers in Stuttgart. Worker dissatisfaction is a key reason in Daimler's decision to abandon Ford production methods.

Avus in suburban Berlin, the first European motor parkway.

British Lord Curzon comments that the Allies floated to victory "on a sea of oil."

1920

Auto accidents are the ninth leading cause of death in the United States, surpassing suicide, measles and cirrhosis.

The United States has 76 cars per 1,000 population, compared to only 5 per 1,000 in Great Britain.

U.S. Congress approves the transfer of 25,000 military surplus trucks and 1,200 caterpillar tractors to state highway departments.

Charleston News and Courier predicts the decline of small villages and growth of larger towns because of highway building.

To the title character of Sinclair Lewis's novel *Babbitt*, the car is "poetry and tragedy, love and heroism."

Minneapolis chapter of the American Automobile Association bans Jews from joining.

William Phelps Eno, the premier U.S. traffic authority, recommends converting public plazas and market squares into parking areas and chopping down street trees that may interfere with tall cars.

Officer William Potts of the Detroit Police Department builds the first modern traffic light (four ways and red-amber-green colors).

Over two million American farmers own autos. They average 7,360 kilometers a year, only about 10 percent for pleasure driving.

More than one million trucks registered in the United States.

U.S. car manufacturers begin to offer heaters as an option.

Ninety million acres, one-quarter of the farmland in the United States, still needed to feed horses.

Amendment to the Minnesota state constitution compels the earmarking of gasoline taxes for road-building.

Recession: 150,000 Detroit auto workers laid off.

G.M. liquidates Samson Tractor Division after losing $42 million in four years.

Dodge becomes the second best-selling American car. Both Dodge brothers die.

The Duponts force Durant out of G.M.

Henry Ford publishes the notorious anti-Semitic forgery, *Protocols of the Elders of Zion,* in the *Dearborn Independent.*

Rolls-Royce opens a factory in Springfield, Massachusetts.

Fabulous new Dusenberg sports cars introduce four-wheel hydraulic brakes and straight eight engines.

Half the automobiles in the world are Model Ts.

Marxist philosopher Antonio Gramsci leads a strike against Fiat in Turin.

Toyo Cork Kogyo, later the maker of Mazda, founded.

Gasoline price increases spur the discovery of new reserves, especially in the Los Angeles basin.

Standard Oil-New Jersey (Exxon) buys the rights to Soviet oil fields from czarist exiles.

1921

Henry Ford, Thomas Edison, Harvey Firestone and Warren G. Harding take a much-publicized auto-camping trip. Warren Harding is the first president to drive his own car.

Royce Hailey's Pig Stand opens in Dallas—the first drive-in restaurant.

First Broadway show based on motor cars—*Six Cylinder Love*.

Anti-segregation meeting of Atlanta blacks passes the resolution: "Buy a car of your own and escape the Jim Crowism of streetcar service."

Los Angeles Police Department arrests the novelist Upton Sinclair for reading the Declaration of Independence on a street corner, reflecting their suspicion of non-automotive street activity.

Newly revitalized Ku Klux Klan adopts autos to hold rallies and terrorize minorities in both the North and South.

Atlanta judge comments: "A large percentage of cases are the result of too much automobile and too little parental control. It is not too much to ask the parents to throw in the clutch and put on the brakes or our entire civilization will take one last joy ride to destruction."

Dupont Company switches from trains to trucks to ship goods.

Major auto sales recession.

After a spat with Henry Ford, William Knudsen moves to G.M., where he revitalizes Chevrolet.

Ford revenges himself on the Leland brothers by buying Lincoln during a liquidity crisis and forces them out.

Ford fires his treasurer for suggesting that Ford Motor Company borrow money, instead compels his dealers to finance him through the recession.

Walter Chrysler buys Maxwell.

Firsts: adjustable front seat, by Hudson; automatic blinking back-up light by Willys-St. Clair; first turbocharger by Mercedes.

Pierce-Arrow is the last U.S. firm to abandon right-hand drive.

Federal Highway Act begins numbering U.S. highways and provides 50 percent matching funds for rural roads in the system. It excludes urban roads, but seeks to link 91 percent of county seats in United States.

Bentley founded.

France issues nationwide traffic regulations.

Jimmy Murphy's Dusenberg is the first American car to win the French Grand Prix.

Czech playwright Karel Capek coins the word "robot."

French architect Le Corbusier plans a mass-produced Citrohan house, a name derived from Citroën. He claims homes can be mass produced on the Fordist model.

U.S. Geological Survey predicts the exhaustion of domestic oil reserves within five years, starting an early energy crisis.

1922

Over 100,000 suburban homes in the United States are wholly auto dependent.

House Beautiful writer complains about the decline of front porch socializing in suburbs: "They have hung their harps upon trees and gone a-motoring."

Auto Club of Southern California does the first modern urban traffic survey in Los Angeles.

Popular song: "You can't afford to marry me, if you can't afford a Ford."

Henry Ford attacks cities as places where "social impurities break out in a festering sore," urges suburbanization.

Public relations flak Samuel Crowther ghost writes Henry Ford's best-selling autobiography, *My Life and Work*.

Innovations: George Frost, a student at Lane High School, Chicago, fits a radio to a car. Crouse-Hinds, a railway signal firm, introduces automatically timed traffic signals in Houston, Texas. Race drivers borrow the idea of seat belts from airplane pilots. Air filter and gas gauge introduced.

Emily Post's best-selling *Etiquette* stirs controversy by sanctioning car driving by unchaperoned single women.

Prado Motors (New York City) imitates aircraft with the propeller-driven Reese Aerocar.

Fifteen million transit car trips carry 417 million passengers into Manhattan. Over 91 million car trips carry 204 million passengers. Thirty-six million pedestrians enter the island.

New York City narrows the park strip in the center of Park Avenue by 50 percent to allow more room for auto traffic.

Ford's associate James Couzens becomes U.S. senator from Michigan.

Assassins murder Irish prime minister Michael Collins in his Leyland Eight touring car.

Cyril Pullin, an Englishman, exceeds 100 mph (160 kph) on a motorcycle.

Vickers (United Kingdom) adds revolving turrets to tanks.

British general Douglas Haig predicts that the tank and truck will not replace the horse.

Austin reduces the power of its basic car from 20 hp to a tax-beating 7 hp. The new Austin 7 is the British Model T, selling 300,000 units in the 1920s.

Citroën offers customers credit on the new 5cv, the French Model T.

Italy's fascist government puts a 122 percent tariff on imported cars.

Lancia Lamba features unit body construction and independent front suspension.

Fifteen-year-old Soichiro Honda, a blacksmith's son, drops out of school, leaves his village (Hamamatsu), for Tokyo, where he hopes to become a mechanic.

Oil discovered in Venezuela.

1923

More cars registered in Kansas than in France and Germany together.

Los Angeles and Salt Lake City have one car for every three people.

More enclosed than open cars sold in the United States for the first time.

Ford's Model T reaches its peak annual production: 1,817,891 units.

Country Club Plaza, the first shopping center, opens in Kansas City.

Realtors register 714 subdivisions with 86,000 lots in Los Angeles. The average lot size is one-fifth acre.

Reformer Elizabeth Boyd Lawton founds the National Committee for the Restriction of Outdoor Advertising.

The United States has its 100,000th auto fatality.

Voters in Los Angeles and Detroit reject transit systems.

Spartanburg, South Carolina—first city to switch to all-bus transit.

Cleveland police arrest a jaywalker. He sues them. Los Angeles police ban jaywalking.

Bronx River Parkway, first public, limited access highway designed for autos, opens. Over 150,000 trees and shrubs have been planted on its route. Suburban Westchester County real estate along its route quadruples in value.

Robert Moses takes over the Long Island State Park Commission, which he will convert to first modern road-building public authority.

Reflective lane markers introduced.

University of Pittsburgh offers the first college course on traffic engineering.

Business groups in New York, Boston and Los Angeles found regional plan associations, in large part to facilitate car travel.

Because student car-owners have a high failure rate, the University of Missouri bans car ownership.

Motor camping advocate writes: "The car or trailer is M'Lord autocamper's castle. . . . The autocamper is a petty feudal monarch in a horizon that is all his own."

Alfred P. Sloan, Jr., becomes president of G.M.

Charles Kettering and Thomas Midgely develop ethyl (leaded) gasoline, which they claim allows a doubling of car mileage.

G.M. introduces an air-cooled, copper engine, a costly flop.

Henry Ford refuses to expand further, fearing antitrust prosecution (according to Charles Sorenson).

Ford worker complains: "If I keep putting on nut No. 86 for 86 more days, I will be nut No. 86 in the Pontiac bughouse."

Automobile companies purchase one-third of the advertising in *Saturday Evening Post*, the best-selling magazine in the United States.

Ford loses the lead in British markets.

Hitler buys his first Mercedes. Ironically, the Mercedes after whom the car was named was Jewish.

Daimler is offering the public 57 different models, an obvious impediment to adopting Ford production methods.

Morris Garages, Oxford, England, builds the first MG.

London authorities blame the soaring fatality rate on the "American speed mania."

Paris adopts U.S.-style traffic lights.

LeMans holds the first 24-hour race for production cars.

Japan encourages motor vehicle imports after the Tokyo earthquake kills hundreds of thousands and destroys rail lines.

Assassins ambush the Dodge of the Mexican revolutionary Pancho Villa, shooting him 12 times.

Cadillacs begin mail service between Beirut and Baghdad.

World oil production tops a trillion barrels: 73 percent in the United States.

Winston Churchill accepts a £50,000 fee to lobby for Shell.

1924

Collier's Magazine reports that Secretary of the Treasury Andrew Mellon wants to move the Washington Monument to create more parking spots in downtown Washington.

Secretary of Commerce Hoover chairs the first National Conference on Street and Highway Safety, which calls for uniform traffic laws.

Average speed of Washington downtown commuters: pedestrians—5.9 kph; drivers—5.7; trolley riders—6.5. Only 20 percent commute by car.

Novelties: White Tower, first fast food hamburger chain, opens. A&W root beer chain also constructs drive-ins, the first to hire "tray girls" to deliver food to cars. Cleveland introduces synchronized traffic signals. Pittsburgh hires the first traffic engineer, Burton Marsh.

In November, 16,833 cars cross the St. John's River into Florida, the beginning of winter motor pilgrimages to Florida.

Los Angeles claims to have the worst traffic jams in the world.

Vogue Magazine cover shows a car customized as a fashion accessory.

Car-customizing is the rage among affluent Parisians.

Walter P. Chrysler produces the first car bearing his name.

Chevrolet ad: "How Can Bolshevism Flourish in a Motorized Country?"

Most new American cars have four-wheel hydraulic brakes. Double fila-ment headlights and Duco lacquer paints (controlled by G.M.) also appear on production cars.

Dodge produces the first all-steel-body closed car.

New G.M. president Alfred Sloan's reorganization creates divisional auton-omy at G.M. He also expands overseas, buying Vauxhall in Great Britain.

Ford, the largest corporate employer of blacks in the United States, with 5,000 black employees, hires its first black salaried employee, engineer James C. Price.

Morris Motors (England) introduces a transfer machine to speed up assembly.

Henry Ford fires the managers of British Ford for allowing their nonunion-ized workers tea breaks and smoking rights.

E. A. Aldridge sets a land speed record of 232 kph on a French *Route Nationale*, the last time this record is set on a road.

Bauhaus leader Walter Gropius suggests that the time has come to mass produce houses, the way Ford mass produces cars.

Berlin adopts American-style traffic lights.

Opel brings the assembly line to Germany for its popular Laubfrosch (tree frog) model.

Soviet motor production begins with ten trucks.

Italy builds the first European highspeed toll road, the Piero Puricelli-de-signed Autostrada, from Milan to Como, Italy. The toll roads have limited access, very few crossroads, and no median divider.

Five workers die in October and 30 are hospitalized after breathing fumes in a plant making leaded gas. *The Nation* notes: "They died in straitjackets. They died stark mad, grinning and gritting their teeth."

Teapot Dome scandal breaks. Oil industrialists had bribed the Harding administration to lease oil reserves set aside for military emergencies.

Low cost Dubbs continuous flow process becomes the norm in refining.

1925

"Saturation point" for the U.S. auto industry, that is, most cars sold are replacements, not first time purchases. Most U.S. families own cars.

Car makers produce the 25-millionth U.S. car. There are more cars than telephones or bathtubs in the United States. The annualized cost of a Model T is less than $2,000 in 1990 dollars.

Ford makes a Model T every 30 seconds, down from 12.9 hours in 1909.

Three-quarters of U.S. cars bought on credit.

Sears-Roebuck establishes a policy of opening new stores only in suburbs.

Regional Plan of New York does the first origin and destination studies and estimates traffic congestion costs in Manhattan at over a million dollars a day.

Syracuse introduces centralized control of downtown traffic lights.

Los Angeles and Washington, D.C., ban horses from downtown.

St. Louis police organize an antispeeding vigilante group.

Local judge sends a frequent speed law violator to a University of Toledo psychology class "for observation."

Judge in Oakland requires a woman speeder to memorize the new California motor vehicle code.

Miller McClintock publishes the first textbook on traffic engineering, *Street Traffic Control*.

Boston and Maine Railroad asks to abandon 1,600 kilometers of rail because of motor vehicle competition.

In *Illinois Railroad Commission v. Duke* the U.S. Supreme Court holds that states cannot regulate interstate trucks.

U.S. highway construction costs exceed $1 billion. Lincoln Highway completed, first transcontinental paved road.

Motor vehicle production is the largest industry in the United States.

Oldsmobile begins to decorate cars with chrome.

Goodyear Tire launches the first advertising blimp.

Citroën installs a 32-meter-high blinking electric advertisement on the Eiffel Tower (taken down in 1936).

Paris bans jaywalking.

France has 40,000 kilometers of paved road, the most in Europe.

Critics of British engineering describe the Bentley as the fastest truck in Europe.

Rolls-Royce adopts the Palladian radiator.

Henry Ford's autobiography becomes a bestseller in Germany. Adolph Hitler, in prison, reads it and later writes: "I am a great admirer of Ford, I shall do my best to put his theories into practice in Germany."

By a vote of 11,318 to 10,271, voters in the Swiss canton of Graubunden end their 25-year-old car ban.

Ford opens an assembly plant in Yokohama, Japan.

Oil and auto industries pack a committee appointed by the surgeon general to investigate the hazards of leaded gasoline. They wrongly, but profitably, conclude that it is harmless.

1926

Over 90 percent of Iowa's farmers own cars. Ten percent of U.S. families own more than one car.

Debate topic for Knights of Columbus meetings: "How can a man be master of an auto, instead of it being his master?

Average daytime travel speed on Fifth Avenue, New York City, drops below 5 kph.

Atlanta merchants complain that downtown business is declining because of traffic jams.

Washington, D.C., installs the first automatically controlled, progressively timed traffic light system on Sixteenth Street.

Washington's traffic director claims a one-third reduction in accidents because of stop signs on side streets and rigorous prosecution of drunk (yes, even during Prohibition) drivers.

Chicago claims that the centrally controlled traffic light system donated to the city by the trolley company has cut travel times in the Loop in half.

Studebaker funds Harvard University's pioneer traffic research program.

Chicago opens Wacker Drive, a double-decked downtown street.

Jeweler's Building (Chicago), the tallest skyscraper west of Manhattan, contains off-street parking for 550 cars.

Peak year for auto fatalities per kilometer of travel in the United States.

Auto accidents are now the fifth leading cause of death in the United States, surpassing syphilis and diabetes.

Nashville Salvation Army estimates that most of the unwed mothers for whom it cares could blame "the predatory drivers of automobiles" for their predicament.

F. Scott Fitzgerald's novel, *The Great Gatsby*, heavily depicts Gatsby's yellow Rolls-Royce with green upholstery as a symbol of both hope and death.

Virginia Liston introduces automotive themes to Blues music with "Rolls-Royce Papa."

San Luis Obispo, California, innkeeper James Vail coins the word, "motel."

Judges in Muncie, Indiana, complain about prostitutes in cars.

University of Illinois prohibits students from owning cars because of accidents, the low academic standing of owners, and the auto's contribution to "moral delinquency."

"XIX," e. e. cummings's poem, compares brand new cars to virgins having their first sexual experience.

Car theft rates are quadruple 1922 levels with a 94 percent recovery rate.

Cannonball Baker drives a truck from New York to San Francisco in less than six days.

Rand-McNally publishes the first U.S. road atlas.

Nation's Traffic, first traffic engineering periodical, founded.

Hollywood car customizer Harley Earl forms G.M.'s Art and Color Section, first Detroit auto styling studio, which begins the annual model change. Oldsmobile had used chrome the previous year and Lincoln hired the LeBaron coach-building firm as stylists.

Pontiac car, with its famous Indian chief hood ornament, introduced by Oakland.

Pierce-Arrow presents the first power steering system; Cadillac the first shatter-resistant ("safety") glass; and AC the mechanical fuel pump and downdraft carburetor.

Well-based, corded, low pressure balloon tires available on new cars.

Ford fires long-time executive Ernest Kanzler for suggesting a six-cylinder engine on the Model T.

Ford introduces the 40-hour work week.

Henry Ford coins the phrase "mass production" in an article written for the *Encyclopedia Britannica*.

First League of Nations road sign convention. It recommends American-style octagonal stop signs and traffic lights. The emphasis is on symbolic signs to overcome language barriers.

Chancellor of the Exchequer Winston Churchill diverts British gas taxes to the general fund. In long run this will lead to a poor British highway system.

Major London traffic reforms include making The Strand one way, requiring one way rotary traffic at Picadilly Circus and lining pedestrian crossings in Parliament Square.

G.M. opens an assembly plant in Japan to avoid a 50 percent tariff.

Soviet leader Leon Trotsky: "The most popular word among our peasants is Fordson."

Ford opens its German subsidiary, building a smaller scale version of the River Rouge plant in Cologne.

British Talbot introduces electric directional signals.

Daimler and Benz merge to form Mercedes-Benz.

4

Peace and War: 1927–1945

1927

Chevrolet, in its first million-sales year, outsells Ford (down to 25% of the U.S. market) for the first time. Three-fourths of cars are sold on credit.

Last (no. 15,007,033) Model T built. Ford adds four-wheel brakes, a major safety improvement, to the new Model A, but takes off the hand brake to save money.

Americans own more cars than telephones.

For the first time more commuters enter downtown Los Angeles by car than public transit.

The United States begins to print ten dollar bills featuring out-of-scale automobiles on traffic-free Pennsylvania Avenue, Washington, D.C., in front of the Treasury Building.

West Side Highway, New York City, first elevated urban highway.

Holland Tunnel, New York City, longest underwater vehicular tunnel—2.61 kilometers—adopts the first lane control signals.

Boston Transportation Study forecasts traffic with a gravity model (travel inversely proportional to the square of the distance between origin and destination).

Pennsylvania Highway Department engineer George Hamlin makes the first accurate estimate of maximum lane capacity—2,000 vehicles an hour at 34 kph. Later analysis refines the figure to 2,200.

Film, *The Jazz Age*, glamorizes joy rides by "flaming youth."

First miniature golf course adorns an American road, Lookout Mountain, Tennessee.

World War I air ace Eddie Rickenbacker becomes president of the Indianapolis Motor Speedway.

American Civic Association sponsors a design competition for roadside stands—won by Pinkie's Pantry, Plainfield, New Jersey.

Self-service A&P grocery chain has grown from 372 outlets in 1916 to 16,000.

Precisionist art show, The Machine Age Exposition, in New York City includes a Studebaker camshaft among its works of art.

Henry Ford apologizes for his anti-Semitic statements.

Chrysler introduces rubber engine mounts.

LaSalle—Harley Earl's first design at G.M.

Franklin makes the last production wood-framed car.

Fageol introduces the modern bus with engine underneath.

Philco begins to market car radios.

G.M. buys Opel, the largest German producer.

French modernist architect Le Corbusier builds a home (Villa Stein, Garches) with a facade dominated by the garage door.

Dancer Isadora Duncan killed when her long, aviation-style scarf catches in her car's rear wheel while driving in France.

Hermann Hesse's surreal novel *Steppenwolf* depicts a war between machines and humans, during which the hero shoots passing motorists and pushes their cars over a cliff.

German director Fritz Lang's film *Spies* features an almost surreal motorcycle chase scene, the first of the highway film noir genre.

Daily Sketch sponsors the first antique car rally from London to Brighton.

Fiat introduces the oil pressure warning light.

Assar Gabrielsson and Gustaf Lavson found Volvo.

Stockholm includes pedestrian controls with its first traffic lights.

Japanese motor vehicle producer Hakuyosha goes bankrupt because of U.S. competition.

Eugene Houdry develops improved catalytic refining process.

1928

First cloverleaf highway intersection, Woodbridge, New Jersey.

University of Chicago sociologist describes the city as suffering from "varicose veins and embolisms" because of traffic jams.

Newly formed American Association of State Highway Officials (AASHO) sets national highway standards (10-foot lanes, 8-foot shoulders, and a concrete thickness of 6 inches), and recommends octagonal stop signs.

Mount Vernon Memorial Highway begun, first aerial photography for highway mapping.

Baltimore borrows a traffic-activated (horn) light from a railroad.

Studebaker buys Pierce-Arrow. Sells it in 1932.

Chrysler takes over Dodge, introduces Plymouth and DeSoto models.

Chrysler decides not to export four-cylinder Dodges to Europe: consumer incomes are too low, gasoline is three times as expensive, and annual horsepower taxes will cost as much as 25 percent of the value of the car.

Cadillac introduces synchromesh transmission, patented in 1924 by independent inventor Earl Thompson, who had been Rube Goldberg's college roommate.

Ford adopts automatic welding to reduce assembly costs. Ultimately, it will make custom coach-building almost impossible.

Henry Ford whines about styling and a Madison Avenue advertising campaign to sell the new Model A: "We are no longer in the automobile, but in the millinery business."

New York Times attacks Ford's employment practices, calling him "the Mussolini of Detroit."

General Motors starts an ad campaign aimed at getting isolated suburban housewives to buy second cars for their families.

Gangster Al Capone spends $30,000 to line his car with boiler plate.

Franklin D. Roosevelt, the polio-stricken governor of New York, buys a Ford customized to operate with only hand controls.

Of 100,000 injured on British roads, 64,000 are pedestrians or bicyclists.

Malcolm Campbell sets the land speed record in his low-slung, streamlined, grilleless Bluebird, prototype for the modern sports car.

Berlin police ban bikes from main streets during workdays, prohibit jaywalking, and allow cars to pass trolleys on right. A newspaper calls for rebuilding the city to allow cars to move faster than pedestrians.

Karl Benz dies at Ladenburg, Germany.

Ferdinand Porsche leaves Daimler-Benz and establishes an independent design firm.

Opel builds an experimental rocket-powered car.

Bauhaus designer Walter Gropius fashions an Art Deco car.

Bavarian Motor Works (BMW) moves from motorcycle to auto production.

Young German engineer Heinz Nordoff, who will preside over Volkswagen's postwar boom, visits Detroit factories.

Ettore Bugatti builds six Royale cars, the largest cars built to date; no royalty ever buys one.

Sakichi Toyoda sells his loom patents for £100,000 to start research into car production. His brother visits Ford's River Rouge plant.

Beijing, China, promises to punish speeders who exceed 24 kph with the death penalty.

Achawcarry Agreement: the seven largest oil companies in the world (Exxon, Socal, Mobil, Gulf, Texaco, British Petroleum, and Royal Dutch Shell—the "Seven Sisters") fix world prices.

1929

Stock market crash triggers a ten-year global depression. At the bottom, in 1933, a quarter of the U.S. work force is unemployed.

Independent luxury car firms control 5 percent of the U.S. market, their peak.

Locomobile, once the largest American car maker, fails. Within ten years, Detroit Electric, Doble, Dupont, Durant, Franklin, Kisell, Marmon, Pierce-Arrow, Reo, Studebaker Stutz, Willys and others will follow suit. Only Studebaker and Willys will limp out of bankruptcy. The shakeout ends independent sports vehicle, electric and steam car production in the United States for decades. Durant's failure will finish William Durant's spectacular automotive financial career.

Forty-four U.S. auto manufacturers still in business.

Detroit replacement parts dealer Alfred O. Dunk presents the National Auto Chamber of Commerce with the blueprints and patents of 756 bankrupt factories that he now owns.

Lynds' *Middletown* reports that the automobile has transformed consumer spending, church attendance and courtship patterns in the United States Battles over driving are a major cause of arguments in families.

Women hold only 24.3 percent of the driver's licenses in the United States.

New York City has 3,000 automatic traffic lights and has cut the traffic squad from 6,000 to 500 officers.

Some state courts accept blood tests as evidence of drunken driving for the first time. Most courts will not admit them as evidence for another ten years and jury trials for drunken driving continue to have a 90 percent acquittal rate.

Architect Clarence Stein builds Radburn, New Jersey, the prototype of auto age subdivision planning (super blocks and cul-de-sacs).

Innovations in roadside architecture: Richard Neutra's Dixie Drive-in Market integrates auto and roadside architecture in modern form, the International Style. A shell-shaped gas station opens in Winston-Salem, North Carolina. Burma Shave begins to erect rhyming billboards. Harlan Sanders opens a gas station in Corbin, Kentucky, later adds a restaurant.

All 48 American states have gasoline taxes reserved for road improvements.

More American commuters ride buses than trolley cars.

Major public festivities celebrate the completion of a paved road between Atlanta and Chattanooga.

Ambassador Bridge (Detroit-Windsor, Ontario)—564 meters.

Chevrolet introduces the "stovebolt six" engine, its response to the powerful, four-cylinder Model A. The engine will serve for 26 years.

Ford builds the first mass-produced station wagons.

In a fit of rage, Henry Ford scraps the six-cylinder engine designed by his son, Edsel.

David Buick dies in poverty in a Detroit hospital.

"Safety" Stutz features vacuum-boosted four-wheel brakes, safety glass and a "no-back" unit for hill holding.

Ford begins its Dagenham, United Kingdom, plant, the largest outside the United States. It will never drop costs to U. S. level because the British market is too small for maximum production. To avoid unions, it pays triple the prevailing wage rate.

Henry Ford refuses to modify his cars for the British market (for example, moving the steering column to the right side), although his share of the market has fallen from 29 percent to 4 percent.

Ford adds handbrakes to the Model A after Germany prohibits its importation for safety reasons.

Mussolini bans Ford's proposed Italian factory.

Enzo Ferrari leaves Alfa-Romeo, starts his firm to build racing cars and make parts.

Ford-Stalin pact: Ford promises to build a Soviet factory.

Morris Minor, a tax-beating 8-hp car, introduced.

British Pedestrian's Association founded, a major anti-auto lobbying group.

Congestion has reduced Paris rush hour traffic speeds to 6 kph.

Russian Ilya Ehrenburg publishes a Marxist novel about the French auto industry, *Life of the Automobile*.

American Petroleum Institute proposes measures to limit oil glut.

Standard Oil-California gets concession in Bahrain, the first U.S. penetration of the Middle East.

British Petroleum decides not to seek oil in Saudi Arabia.

1930

Almost all families (94%) in Los Angeles live in single-family homes.

U.S. census shows that factory employment in the last ten years has increased in suburbs, declined in central cities.

Impact of the auto on Boston since 1925: downtown property values have declined by $34 million, values in outlying neighborhoods up by $76 million.

Census data suggest that southern cities are becoming more racially segregated as car-owning whites move to suburbs that have no public transportation.

Kansas City survey shows that the auto is twice as fast as the trolley, door-to-door, for suburban commuters.

Institute of Traffic Engineers founded.

King Cullen, first supermarket, Queens, New York City. Supermarkets are an outgrowth of the auto age, because pedestrians cannot carry large amounts of groceries home.

Detroit's population is 1.8 million, six times 1900 level.

Edward Bassett coins the word "freeway" for urban roads designed for trucks, as well as the passenger cars allowed on parkways.

Engineer Franklin Pillsbury projects Route 128, Boston, the first suburban beltway.

Around this date both German and American engineers begin to tailor roads to specific speeds.

Cadillac introduces the first V-16 automobile engine. President Hoover buys one to replace the White House Pierce-Arrow. Bugatti and Marmon also build some V-16s.

Police departments start putting radios in cars.

G.M. acquires two locomotive manufacturers, will only ship cars on railroads buying G.M. locomotives.

Two-thirds of Ford dealers are in rural areas.

Michelin closes its U.S. factory.

National Auto Chamber of Commerce announces a plan to spend $10 million removing unsafe older cars from the road.

Britain eliminates the speed limit. Over the next four years accident mortality climbs 50 percent.

British car registration passes one million mark.

British *Army Quarterly* attacks "the garage army" and predicts: "The next war will principally [be] fought and won by men on their feet."

Paris, with the highest traffic densities in Europe, bans parking from many downtown streets, begins forcing horses off the streets, and starts replacing trolleys with buses. Most narrow streets are already one way.

East Texas oil field opened.

1931

Fifty millionth U.S. vehicle produced.

New York City driver knocks down, but does not injure seriously, jaywalking British politician Winston Churchill on Fifth Avenue.

Highland Park Shopping Village in Dallas, the first mall with stores facing away from the street.

Concrete building industry awards a prize to a Riverhead, Long Island, restauranteur who has put up a theriomorphic roadside building in the shape of a duck. The diner will play a major role in the emergence of postmodern architecture in the 1970s.

Radio-controlled garage door openers become available.

Southern California adolescents begin to hold drag races and "chicken" games on the dry lake beds of the region. Fords are the preferred cars.

G.M.-built refrigerated truck delivers fruit from California to New York City in 117 hours.

George Washington Bridge, New York—1,067 meters.

Caterpillar begins to market diesel-powered tractors.

René Clair, *A Nous La Liberté*, first film to satirize the assembly line.

Poet e. e. cummings claims to have been stranded on a traffic island in the Place de la Concorde, Paris, for 2 and 1/2 hours.

First cross–English Channel car ferry.

Clarence Stein discusses Radburn at the International Housing and Town Planning Conference in Berlin.

Ford builds an assembly plant in Germany.

Daimler-Benz begins massive truck sales in the Soviet Union.

Rolls-Royce closes its U.S. factory, buys Bentley.

Morris Minor, the first British car to cost less than £100, now advertised as having 100 mph (160 kph) speed and 100-mpg (42.7 kpl) gas efficiency.

Mercedes introduces independent front suspension. G.M. follows in 1934, Ford in 1949.

Toyo Kogyo sells the first Mazdas (named after the Zoroastrian god of light), three-wheel trucks.

Tokyo installs a progressive light system on the Ginza.

Britain puts a 40 percent tax on gasoline.

Texas Railroad Commission rations oil production to stabilize prices. This alleged conservation measure favors the large producers.

1932

One-room rural schools decline because school districts operate 63,000 school buses in the United States.

Most (86%) of a sample of 64 executives working in Newark live in the suburbs.

New York City begins to replace its trolleys with buses.

Car registration down 10 percent from 1929 levels in the United States because of the depression. One newspaper comments: "Many a family that has lost its car, has found its soul."

Sociologist reports on small town funerals in Montana, where the motorcade is arranged by status, that is, Lincolns first and Model Ts last.

James Cagney plays a misogynist race driver in Howard Hawks's classic film, *The Crowd Roars*.

National Highway Users Conference, a lobbying group including auto manufacturers, truckers, oil companies, teamsters and road builders, formed.

Ford closes 23 of his 31 assembly plants. Only 8 ever reopen. By this date Ford's U.S. market share has declined to 26 percent. In 1931 the firm lost $500 million.

Ford cuts his minimum wage from $7 to $4 a day. Black workers in the Inkster, Michigan, plant are only paid $1, receiving the rest of their pay in scrip redeemable only at a company store.

Ford Hunger March, beginning of massive labor unrest in 1930s Detroit. Ford builds machine gun towers at River Rouge.

Drop frame construction generally introduced in the United States, allows lower-slung cars.

Oldsmobile introduces the Stromberg automatic choke.

Cadillac adopts the extended rear deck.

Ford markets the first V-8 engine on a low-priced car. It will become the preferred motor for street racing for more than 20 years.

Engineer Thomas Agg's concept of discomfort criteria to design curves widely adopted by most texts, implying broader curves and better sightlines.

State College High School (Pennsylvania) offers the first driver education program in the United States.

Aldous Huxley sets his best-selling, anti-utopia *Brave New World* in a futuristic world where years are dated a.f. (after Ford) or b.f. (before Ford), and where Ford's autobiography has replaced the Bible.

William Morris, the car manufacturer, gives Oswald Moseley £50,000 to found a British fascist party.

Ford of England begins to market the Popular, a small car built to European standards, that will soon be sold for less than £100.

Estimated peak of German bicycle usage (30% of urban traffic, 35 million bikes registered).

German engineers do early experiments on auto aerodynamics.

Ferdinand Porsche patents torsion bar suspension, which makes independently suspended rear wheels and rear engines possible.

DeDion-Bouton makes its last car.

Stalin opens the Ford-designed Gorky Auto Works, the largest auto factory in Europe. It adopts production machinery made for the old Model A.

Oil discovered in Bahrain.

King Saud sells Arabian oil concession to Standard Oil-California to counterbalance the British dominance of the Middle East.

Smoot-Hawley Tariff taxes imported oil at 32 cents a barrel.

Venezuela becomes Britain's largest oil supplier.

1933

Cars entering the central business district daily: Los Angeles—277,000; Chicago—113,000; Boston—66,000.

Richard Hollingshead opens the first drive-in movie, on Admiral Wilson Boulevard, Camden, New Jersey.

Covered Wagon Company (Detroit) begins mass production of mobile homes.

Midget cars, which will save American auto racing during the depression, introduced at Sacramento, California.

Montauk, New York, gas station shaped as a lighthouse wins a local architectural prize.

Frank Redford builds the first in his Wigwam Village roadside cabin chain, featuring units shaped like teepees (built with stucco over a steel frame).

Edsel Ford commissions Diego Rivera's powerful mural, *Detroit Industry*, a socialist-realist depiction of assembly line work.

Chevrolet covers the radiator with a grille and introduces the fender skirt.

Ford imitates G.M., adopts the annual model change.

Accelerator and starter pedals combined.

Bank robber Clyde Barrow recommends stealing Ford V-8s for getaway cars.

Unemployed bricklayer Joe Zangara fires at president-elect Franklin Roosevelt in a light blue Buick limousine in Miami, misses Roosevelt, but kills Mayor Anton Cermak of Chicago.

Pierce Silver Arrow, supposedly "born in the wind tunnel and made by hand," is a major hit at the Chicago World's Fair. Even in the depression, car fantasies continue.

Studebaker's president commits suicide after the firm enters bankruptcy.

Detroit firms ignore Section 7a of the National Industrial Recovery Act, which requires collective bargaining with employees.

Franklin Roosevelt approves the Home Owners Loan Corporation. It will make mortgages for suburban homes easier to get but will begin "red-lining" of central city housing, guaranteeing urban decay.

Architect Buckminster Fuller granted a patent on a futuristic streamlined, three-wheel Dymaxion car. The prototype kills three people in an accident.

U.S. Congress passes the Hayden-Cartwright Act, which requires states to segregate gasoline taxes for road-building if they want federal highway aid.

Henry Ford maneuvers the failure of Detroit's two largest banks to revenge himself for social and political snubs by the old social elite that control them.

In his historical novel, *U.S.A.*, John Dos Passos writes that Henry Ford only paid his famous $5-a-day wage "to good, clean American workmen, who don't drink or smoke cigarettes or think or read."

Hitler accelerates Dr. Fritz Todt's autobahn building projects in Germany.

Hitler orders standardized parts for all German cars, hurting Ford, which imports U.S. parts, but not G.M.-owned Opel.

Hitler commissions Volkswagen, literally "people's car," from Ferdinand Porsche, after noting that the Model T "destroys class differences" in the United States. Hitler never learned to drive.

At the request of Daimler-Benz, a leading financier of the Nazi party, Hitler ends luxury taxes on autos. Benz drops the Jewish members of its board of directors.

I. G. Farben, the German chemical giant, develops synthetic rubber.

Il Traffico Urban (Milan), first European traffic engineering periodical.

William Gorham, an American engineer, designs the first Nissan car, a copy of the Austin Seven.

1934

Peak year for auto fatalities per motor vehicle in the United States—over 15,000 pedestrians killed.

Oscar-winning comedy, *It Happened One Night*, has romantic road-as-escape and hitch-hiking themes.

Gangster John Dillinger steals his first Ford V-8.

First parking ramp opens—Boston.

American Federation of Labor (AFL) charters the United Auto Workers.

Aerodynamically shaped Air Flow Chrysler with built-in headlights is introduced, but rejected, by public. One-third of its engine mass is ahead of the front axle, a novelty that improves handling.

Graham pioneers the supercharger on production cars.

Westinghouse's all electric House of Tomorrow at the Chicago World's Fair features an electric garage door opener.

First diesel bus in the United States.

Robert Moses builds the Meadowbrook Parkway, the first entirely divided, entirely limited access highway in the world.

Vatican officials attack a Fiat advertisement as too sensual.

Mersey Tunnel, United Kingdom—3.43 kilometers, longest underwater vehicular tunnel.

Morris becomes the first British-owned car firm with a moving assembly line.

British Road Traffic Bill mandates insurance, driver's tests, imposes a 30-mph (48 kph) speed limit, establishes pedestrian crossings and bans jaywalking.

Cost of developing the first mass-produced front wheel drive car nearly bankrupts Citroën. Andre Citroën loses control to Michelin.

Croat nationalists kill King Alexander of Yugoslavia and Foreign Minister Louis Barthou of France in their Mercedes in Marseilles.

First Datsun (export name of Nissan) shipped.

Emir of Kuwait gives the concession for newly discovered oil resources to Kuwait Oil (50% Gulf, 50% British Petroleum).

1935

Motor vehicle ownership per 1,000 population: United States—205; France—49; United Kingdom—45; Germany—16; USSR—1.

Americans request over 35 million reprints of J. C. Furnas's ". . . and Sudden Death," a *Reader's Digest* article with nothing but gory descriptions of car accidents.

Automobile Manufacturer's Association founds the Automotive Safety Foundation, which emphasizes driver education, ignoring vehicle safety.

Detroit plastic surgeon Clarence Straith, tired of patching the faces of accident victims, puts a padded dashboard, recessed control knobs, and seat belts in his own car.

Carlton Magee devises the first parking meter in Oklahoma City. Rev. C. H. North is the first person ticketed for a violation.

Elmo Roper begins to take "scientific" public opinion polls for U.S. newspapers. Three-fourths of those surveyed assert that auto ownership is a necessity.

Dallas survey shows 75 percent of motel visits are very short time stays by couples.

Elvis Presley born at home in Tupelo, Mississippi, because his family lacks a car and their doctor does not believe in driving his patients to the hospital. Most American babies will not be born in hospitals until 1938.

Works Progress Administration counts 35,000 mobile homes in Florida, a hint of things to come.

New York City replaces most of its trolleys with buses.

Frank Bartell rides to a bicycle record of 80.5 mph on a straight line.

Blues musician Sleepy John Estes sings about the Model T Ford as the friend of the poor, suggesting that ownership of used cars is becoming increasingly common in impoverished black communities.

Barney Oldfield arranges the first auto stunt show in Chicago.

Antique Automobile Club of America founded.

More than 1.6 million kilometers (one million miles) of roads in the United States have a paved surface.

Chevrolet sells its ten millionth car.

G.M. and Studebaker introduce steel roofs.

U.S. government begins to regulate truck safety.

United Auto Workers (UAW) holds its first convention and joins the John L. Lewis-headed Conference of Industrial Organizations (CIO), an affiliate of the AFL.

Over 2,000 trucks purchased from Ford-U.S. ease Mussolini's Ethiopian invasion.

German government subsidies help Mercedes dominate the Grand Prix racing circuit.

Grand Prix driver Tazio Nuvolari develops the four wheel drift cornering technique.

T. E. Lawrence (Lawrence of Arabia) killed in a motorcycle crash.

Jaguar, a maker of motorcycle sidecars, debuts the 2.7 Liter Saloon.

"Big Three" French producers agree not to produce mini-cars.

Volvo markets a Chrysler Air Flow look-alike.

1936

North Carolina sociologist notes that auto ownership allows sharecropping blacks to escape the rigid social control of their communities.

Robert Johnson's hit blues song, "Terraplane Blues," describes a Hudson car as a woman.

Charlie Chaplin's film *Modern Times* satirizes assembly line work.

Antique Automobile, the first car restoration periodical, founded.

Dodge engineer W. E. Blandenburg's experimental seat belt saves him in a roll-over test designed to show the car's safety.

New York Governor Herbert Lehman proposes putting speed governors in the cars of those convicted of reckless driving.

Automobile Manufacturer's Association promises not to emphasize speed in advertisements.

Chrysler is first to offer defroster vents.

Cord offers pop-up headlamps.

Ford slips to third place in U.S. sales.

Estate lawyers create the Ford Foundation as a means to avoid inheritance taxes. It will save Henry Ford's heirs $36 million in inheritance taxes.

"Great sit-down" at the G.M. Flint, Michigan, complex begins auto industry unionization. Workers celebrate the victory with a motorcade.

California's Department of Public Works opposes trolley routes on state-funded roads, arguing that streetcars cause congestion.

First stock car races at Daytona.

Mercedes markets the first production diesel car.

Fiat mass produces the 18-kpl, 83-kph, 13-hp Torpolino ("Little Mouse"). In next 18 years, 590,000 will be sold.

Ford appeases Hitler by firing the manager of its German subsidiary because he has a Jewish ancestor.

Opel offers to build the Volkswagen, but Hitler rejects the proposal because G.M. owns Opel.

Hitler begins a synthetic fuel program.

With the support of France's Popular Front government the French union, CGT, organizes Renault, Citroën and Peugeot, in a strike wave featuring sit-downs.

Soichiro Honda retires from race car driving after sustaining major injuries in a crash.

Japanese government licenses Toyota and Nissan as independent companies. Almost all their production is trucks. Toyoda family chooses to name their firm Toyota because it is easier to pronounce.

1937

Southern California Timing Association founded—the onset of organized drag racing.

Architectural Record notes the triumph of garages integrated into houses and the decline of the front porch.

Los Angeles Auto Club issues its highway plan, the basis for the L.A. freeway system. Traffic jams are causing "stagnation and atrophy."

Lewis Gannett complains that Yosemite National Park is as crowded with traffic as New York City.

First drive-in bank—Vernon, California.

Sylvan Goodman builds the first shopping cart, Oklahoma City.

Blues singer Bessie Smith, injured in an auto accident in Mississippi, dies of shock after the nearest hospital refuses to treat her because she is black.

Institute of Traffic Engineers reports that seven high schools scattered around the United States offer driver education.

New York City freezes the number of taxi medallions.

Congress passes the Wagner Act, authorizing federally sponsored union elections.

UAW organizes auto plants throughout the U.S. car industry, except Ford. Ford goons brutally beat union organizers at the "Battle of the Overpass."

CIO breaks away from the AFL.

William Knudsen becomes president of General Motors. Alfred Sloan becomes chairman of the board.

G.M.'s Art and Color section renamed the Styling Section.

Firsts on U.S. production cars: automatic transmission—Oldsmobile; gearshift lever moved to the steering column, iridescent auto paints become available and first windshield washers—Studebaker.

New York, Connecticut and Rhode Island legislatures allow road builders to limit abutter access. Traffic in and out of roadside strips on boulevard-style highways have destroyed their value as traffic movers.

Merritt Parkway, the first limited access, inter-city road in the United States, completed, from New York to Hartford.

Congress rejects Roosevelt's plan to build coast-to-coast toll "super-high-ways."

Lloyd Aldrich, Los Angeles's city engineer and highway planner, visits the Westchester and Long Island parkway systems, which set the design standards that will be adopted for freeways.

Lincoln Tunnel, New York City, longest underwater vehicular tunnel—4.0 kilometers.

Golden Gate Bridge, San Francisco—1,280 meters.

Britain imposes a 67.7 percent tax on new cars.

Volkswagen Corporation formed with government capital. Its president, Ferdinand Porsche, visits Henry Ford and recruits some German-American auto workers.

German economists estimate that the auto and road-building industries have generated one million new jobs since Hitler took over.

Pininfarina designs a streamlined Lancia with an aerodynamic shape including a sloped radiator and curved windshield. He adds "torpedo" mudguards the following year.

Italian government buys Alfa-Romeo.

Pierre Michelin dies in a car crash.

Britain requires safety glass on autos.

1938

Cadillac surpasses Packard as the best-selling American luxury car.

Cadillac 60 Special eliminates running boards, allowing a wider seat.

Harley Earl falls in love with a prototype of the P-38 airplane.

Chrysler offers fluid drive transmission.

Ford introduces its first Mercury cars.

Because commuters are switching from rail to car and shoppers are choosing suburban stores, the number of persons entering Philadelphia's central business district is down 11 percent in the last ten years, while auto traffic is up 52 percent. Boston, Detroit, St. Louis and Pittsburgh report similar patterns.

New York City survey shows 33 percent of the pedestrians killed in traffic accidents are drunk.

Donald Davidson, a southern traditionalist, describes the new roadside architecture: "A modernistic rash among the water oaks and Spanish moss."

First account of the folkloric story of a car sold very cheaply because its owner had died in it appears in the black community of Mecosta, Michigan. It will spread to Detroit by 1944 and England by 1951.

Ford thugs seek to kidnap UAW leader Walter Reuther from his apartment. In a transparent miscarriage of justice, they are acquitted.

Right wing House Un-American Activities Committee labels Walter Reuther and 300 other union leaders as subversives.

Schell Program reorganizes German truck production along military lines.

Hitler awards Henry Ford the Grand Cross of the Supreme Order of the German Eagle.

Germany plans a new town for Volkswagen workers (originally "Town of the Strength through Joy Car," later Wolfsburg) after Radburn, New Jresry.

Paris replaces its last trolley cars with buses.

Oil found in Saudi Arabia.

1939

German blitzkrieg in Poland shows the advantage of mechanized warfare.

Ford plants in British Commonwealth converted to war production.

Ford of Germany begins to manufacture trucks for the Wehrmacht.

German government takes over G.M.'s subsidiary, Opel, which produces the Kadett, the top-selling car in Europe.

Attempts of G.M.-Japan to merge with Nissan or Toyota fail. The Japanese military force Ford and G.M. to close their factories, which had already built 250,000 trucks for the Japanese army.

John Steinbeck's *Grapes of Wrath* depicts a migrant farm worker family, whose life centers on their Hudson. He describes the tractors that plow over their land as "snub-nosed monsters . . . raping methodically, raping without passion."

Dorothea Lange publishes her famous photo collection of migrant workers on the road, *American Exodus*.

U.S. Route 1 has 300 gas stations, 500 billboards, 400 other drive-in businesses and 200 intersections in the 50 miles between New York and Trenton. There are over 1,000 billboards between Washington and Baltimore.

FBI director J. Edgar Hoover denounces motels as "camouflaged brothels."

In the previous three years, Detroit property owners have leveled 96 downtown buildings for parking lots. Landholders in other cities follow suit, as automobility and the depression reduce the value of downtown buildings.

Lewis Mumford's film, *The City*, and G.M.'s exhibit, *Futurama* (designed by Norman Bel Geddes), at the 1939 World's Fair forecast societies built around the auto and limited access highways.

Indianapolis 800 requires crash helmets for drivers.

Auto industry begins to lobby for urban freeways. Studebaker president Paul Hoffman tells *Saturday Evening Post* readers: "We must dream of gashing our way ruthlessly through built-up sections of overcrowded cities."

U.S. Bureau of Public Roads director Thomas MacDonald opposes limited access interstate freeways, arguing that there is insufficient traffic to justify them, underestimates by a factor of nine likely traffic on the planned Pennsylvania Turnpike.

Howard Johnson builds the first of his orange-roofed restaurants outside New England with a popular operation across the street from the World's Fair.

Buick introduces flashing electric turn signals in the United States, 24 years after they were invented.

Nash offers air conditioning as an option.

Oil company boycott ends exports of newly nationalized Mexican oil. Mexico will not fully regain its international trade until the 1970s.

1940

Motorized German blitzkrieg conquers France in six weeks, despite the fact that France has 20 percent more tanks and 100 percent more trucks. The Germans, fearing a fuel shortage, plan to move supplies to infantry divisions with 2.7 million horses. After surrender the French turn 700,000 motor vehicles over to the Germans.

Volkswagen's slave laborers begin war production of jeeplike vehicles. Over 336,000 Germans will lose $67 million in prewar deposits for Volkswagens, probably the largest consumer fraud ever.

George Raft and Humphrey Bogart star in *They Drive by Night*, the first trucking movie.

Henry Fonda stars in the film version of *Grapes of Wrath*. Stalin will ban the movie because the message Soviet audiences get is not that many Americans are desperately poor, but that even the poorest Americans can afford cars.

Racist Natchez, Mississippi, restaurant owner advertises with a seven-meter-tall roadside sculpture of a black "mammy."

Pennsylvania Turnpike, first modern U.S. long-distance toll road, opens. Modeled on the German autobahns, it has no speed limit.

Arroyo Seco Parkway, Los Angeles, opens. When its name is changed to freeway the following year, it suggests a major change in urban highway functions. There are no tolls, and it is open to trucks, unlike the New York area parkways on which it is modeled.

Survey data show that tickets can be fixed easily in 39 of the 76 largest cities in the United States.

Most U.S. justices of the peace (J.P.) are paid from fines. Traffic violators are convicted 98 percent of the time in their hearings. One J.P. claims that he had earned $4,553 the previous year from just one traffic light. J.P.s have a 98 percent conviction rate, much higher than the 80 percent rate in municipal traffic courts.

Wilbur Shaw drives his Boyle Special (actually a Maserati that is not competitive in European road races) to victory in the Indianapolis 800-km race for the second year in a row.

Over 100,000 buses in the United States.

Walter Chrysler dies.

Henry Ford, still an isolationist, reneges on a deal to build aircraft engines for Britain. His son, Edsel, finally secures his reluctant consent to build bombers for the United States.

Packard wins the contract that Ford canceled to build 6,000 Rolls-Royce aircraft engines for the Royal Air Force.

Henry Ford tells reporters that "International Jewish bankers" caused the European war.

G.M. shuts down its LaSalle division.

Harley Earl commits G.M. to "torpedo" bodies.

G.M. head William Knudsen leads the U.S. industrial preparedness effort.

U.S. government begins to plan for rubber stockpiling.

Engineer Karl Pabst of Willys builds a new four wheel drive military vehicle, named the "Jeep," after a Popeye cartoon character.

Sealed beam headlights introduced. Not standard until 1956.

G.M. begins to offer hydramatic automatic transmissions developed by Earl Thompson on most makes: "It is here! A car without a clutch pedal, a car that never needs shifting . . . , the most modern car in the world."

Autobahn engineers Hans Lorenz and Fritz Heller develop a mathematical model for designing modern highway curves.

World oil production tops two trillion barrels, 65 percent in the United States.

1941

Nazi Germany delays its invasion of the Soviet Union to secure Rumanian oil fields, likely a fatal mistake.

Germany's 4,000 tanks destroy the Soviet Union's 17,000 tanks.

Einsatzgruppen, Nazi death squads, begin to kill Jews in German-occupied Russia with truck exhaust fumes.

Hitler's autobahn network completed—2,122 kilometers.

The United States embargoes oil shipments to Japan. Japan's measured response is to bomb Pearl Harbor.

Japan cuts off Far East rubber supplies to the United States.

UAW (and the American labor movement in general) promise no strikes for duration of war. Reuther wants auto factories to build "500 planes a day."

On the outbreak of war with the United States, Germany takes over Ford factories in Germany.

Volkswagen, which commits less than half its capacity to the war effort, continues to make civilian sedans.

In *A New England* the British planner S. D. Adshead is the first to suggest price rationing for downtown traffic entry.

U.S. Supreme Court rules that states may mandate insurance.

Village of Larchmont, New York, opens the first metered parking lot, near its commuter rail station.

Ford recognizes the UAW.

Henry Ford develops an experimental "soybean" car. The idea fails because plastic derived from soybeans is more expensive than steel for body parts.

Antitrust prosecutors force G.M. to allow purchasers to borrow from other credit sources besides GMAC. Ford and Chrysler agree to the same terms.

Cadillac offers factory-installed air conditioning as an option.

Cadillac fenders flow through the door.

Nash markets a car with seats that convert into a bed.

Futuristic Chrysler Thunderbolt, a prototype, features retractable headlights, electric windows, and electric locks—only six made.

R. M. Langer predicts nuclear-powered plastic cars in *Collier's Magazine*.

Atlanta's City Planning Commission again proposes a "greenbelt" parkway to stop expansion of the black ghetto.

Fourteen-year-old Chuck Berry buys a 1934 Ford V-8 for $35 ($5 down).

First *Tom Swift* series ends after six ghostwriters have written 41 books. Adolescents can no longer identify with Swift, now a married, millionaire industrialist.

Largest scientific research team ever assembled develops a fluidized catalytic cracking process for Standard Oil of New Jersey.

1942

War forces a U.S. national speed limit, 35 mph (56 kph), and gasoline rationing, primarily to save on rubber.

Auto engineer Hugh DeHaven publishes the first studies of the impact of crashes on humans, basing his *War Medicine* article on pathology studies of suicidal jumpers. The study suggests that people in cars or planes can survive much higher impact speed than previously thought.

Congress forces Standard Oil of New Jersey to release synthetic rubber patents developed by I. G. Farben, but held off the market.

Henry Ford, in his dotage, believes that President Roosevelt plans to assassinate him.

Military engineers build the 2,400-kilometer Alcan (Washington-Alaska) highway.

U.S. depression relief agency, the Works Progress Administration, shuts down after building or surfacing 1,041,600 kilometers of road.

False sightings of Japanese aircraft lead to panic in Los Angeles, where anti-aircraft gunners fire off 1,400 rounds of ammunition. The "air raid" triggers one of the worst traffic jams in Los Angeles history, because traffic and street lights are shut off.

Secret Service armor-plates FDR's Cadillac, adding bulletproof glass and tires.

British agents assassinate Mercedes-riding Rudolph Heyderich, Nazi procurator of Czechoslovakia, triggering bloody reprisals.

Daimler-Benz leads German industry in slaves, now 40 percent of its work force. Because of Nazi policies "protecting" women, it employs fewer women workers than in World War I.

Manager of Benz's Reichsof factory shoots three Jewish slaves who hesitate to carry out a work order. Benz opens ethnically segregated brothels for slave laborers from Nazi-occupied countries.

Ferdinand Porsche designs the Tiger tank.

Heinrich Himmler's *Guidelines for Planning and Design of Cities in the East* include bikeways and separate pedestrian paths.

General Rommel orders his troops to try to capture "any Ford vehicle."

The Soviets have increased their annual tank production from 6,000 to 24,000 tanks since 1940.

G.M. builds an assembly plant in Iran, which will assemble 184,000 trucks for the Soviets by war's end.

1943

Because of wartime housing shortages, over half a million Americans live in mobile homes.

September 8: first L.A. smog crisis.

Edsel Ford dies. The U.S. military discharges his son, Henry Ford II, hoping that he can prevent further mismanagement of war production by Henry Ford, Sr.

Stout announces plans to market a flying automobile after the war.

Whites, angered by black migration to wartime jobs in Detroit, trigger a race riot. The UAW advocates workplace integration, but "hate strikers" dominate some plants.

While lunging for the USSR's oil fields in the Caucasus, Hitler's armies expose their flank to a counterattack from the north and are crushed in the most decisive battle of the war—Stalingrad.

I. G. Farben chemical cartel produces 75 percent of Germany's gas from coal. Farben employs many slaves (mostly POWs and Jews).

Germany switches most domestic vehicles (and a few tanks) to wood, charcoal or peat fuel burned in Imbert generators.

Jean-Pierre Peugeot pays a British spy 100,000 francs to avoid bombing of his factory, allows selected sabotage.

London's new city plan calls for a ring road (finished 50 years later) and freezing downtown development to solve the traffic crisis.

Communist Leo Lenfranco leads a walkout at the Fiat factory in Turin, which rapidly turns into an antiwar general strike.

Venezuela gets the first "50%-50%" oil deal.

1944

On the verge of encircling a German army, General George Patton's tanks run out of gasoline.

Because Allied bombing reduced German fuel production by 95 percent between March and September, Panzer units run out of gas during the Battle of the Bulge.

At government insistence, Ford of England recognizes a union for the first time.

Congress creates the V.A. Loan Program—a key U.S. subsidy to postwar suburbanization.

G.M. subsidiary buys the L.A. street railway system, planning to replace trolleys with G.M.-built buses.

American Automobile Association opposes parking meters as "just another tax."

City planner Robert Moses urges the repeal of the New York State law banning parking meters in cities of one million population.

DeGaulle's Free French government nationalizes Renault for its collaboration with the Germans. Louis Renault dies after a beating in a French jail.

1945

Detroit's wartime production: 49,000 tanks, 126,000 armored cars, 2,600,000 trucks, 27,000 airplanes and 5,947,000 guns.

Ford's British wartime production: 301,000 vehicles; German wartime production (in government-controlled factories, still administered by Ford executives): 102,000 vehicles. The slave-operated German plants use machinery looted from Ford of France. Ford also makes flamethrowers for the German army.

Ford and G.M. factories made 70 percent of Germany's wartime trucks.

Newly liberated slaves (mostly prisoners of war) seek to burn down the Volkswagen plant in Wolfsburg. U.S. Army saves it.

Red Army confiscates G.M.'s Opel plant, ending its supremacy among German auto makers.

G.M. announces that it made $12.3 billion worth of military supplies during the war at a $673 million profit.

By war's end, the United States has provided the Soviets with 345,000 motor vehicles.

General George Patton killed in a car crash in Germany.

For the first time most U.S. roads are paved.

Ford resumes auto production five weeks before V-J Day.

Henry Ford's wife and daughter-in-law force him to resign as president of Ford by threatening to sell their stock to outsiders. His grandson, Henry Ford II, becomes president. He discovers that the firm keeps its entire reserve ($700 million) in cash in a vault.

John Steinbeck's popular novel, *Cannery Row*, claims that most 1920s babies were conceived in Model T Fords.

Life Magazine takes note of the hot rod culture of Los Angeles adolescents.

Anton "Tony" Hulman buys the Indianapolis Motor Speedway, reinvigorates the famous 800-kilometer race.

Soviets begin to develop Trans-Ural oil fields.

Aramco (a largely American-owned consortium) brings in the giant Ghawar (Saudi Arabia) oil deposits, which cost 50 cents a barrel to produce, compared to $1 for Texas oil.

An early hard-surface street, cobblestones with a brick wheelway, Washington, D.C., c. 1889. From author's collection.

Frederick Law Olmsted built the first grade-separated urban streets in the Transverses through Central Park, 1857. Photo courtesy of Dona McShane.

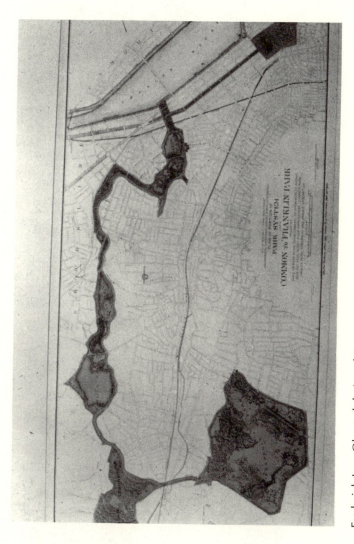

Frederick Law Olmsted designed Boston's "Emerald Necklace," the first comprehensive, limited-access parkway system, 1874. From Boston Park Commission Report.

Rural roads still were morasses in the spring as late as 1940 when this photo was taken by the Farm Security Administration in Pie Town, New Mexico. Photo courtesy of the Library of Congress.

The first highway exit ramp on the Charles River Speedway (Boston, 1898), which allowed fast-moving vehicles to slow down before joining slower traffic. The lanes on the left were reserved for fast-moving trotters. From the *Engineering News-Record.*

In 1914 the twice-daily traffic jam became the norm in most large American cities. This is Fifth Avenue, near 42nd Street, claimed to be the busiest intersection in the world. From *American City Magazine.*

Cities responded to early traffic jams, first with traffic police, then "crow's nests" and finally traffic lights. All three were being used on this Detroit intersection in 1915. Photo courtesy of the Library of Congress.

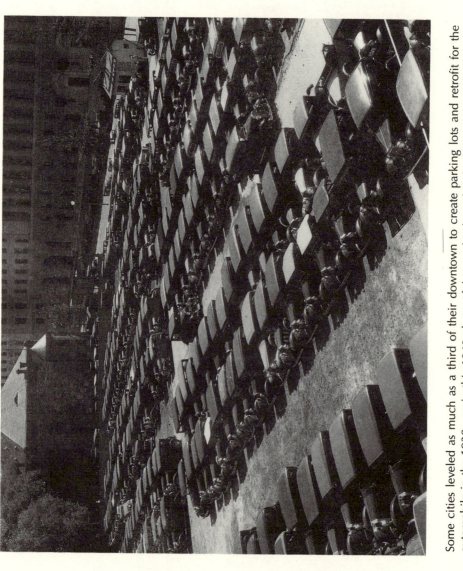

Some cities leveled as much as a third of their downtown to create parking lots and retrofit for the automobile in the 1930s, as in this 1940 photo of the newly cleared Federal Triangle in Washington. Photo courtesy of the Library of Congress.

During the 1920s the suburban roadside rapidly became cluttered with billboards and drive-in businesses, such as this road outside Washington, D.C., in Virginia. Note that roadside lodgings were segregated. From *American City Magazine*.

The 1921 Federal Highway Act helped finance good four-lane roads like Route 1 in New Jersey. Their suburban sections speedily became jammed as car owners flocked to new subdivisions. From *American City Magazine*.

The Bronx River Parkway (1923) embodied most of the modern concepts of highway design: limited access, grade separation, lane division and user fees. From the Westchester County Park Commission.

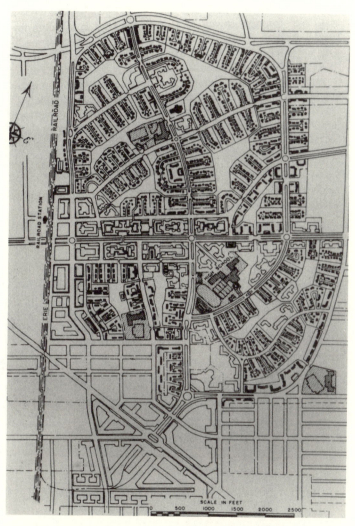

In 1929 architect Clarence Stein planned the prototype auto age suburban tract, Radburn, New Jersey, with super-blocks, curvilinear streets and cul de sacs. From *American City Magazine.*

The exodus from the rural South to California or to big cities could end in disaster if the car broke down, as happened to these Okies in 1936. From the Farm Security Administration.

New Jersey's Highway Department built the first cloverleaf intersection in Woodbridge in 1929. From the New Jersey Highway Department.

5

The Age of Muscle and Smog: 1946–1964

1946

Robert Penn Warren's *All the King's Men* notes the impact of cars on southern culture: "Sugar-boy couldn't talk, but he could express himself when he got his foot on an accelerator." One character says of the car's effect on families: "A man could just git up and git, if'n a notion came on him."

Alienated World War II veterans start the Hell's Angels motorcycle gang in the blue collar Los Angeles suburb of Fontana.

Nat "King" Cole Trio introduces the Bobby Troupe song "Route 66," later remade by the Andrews Sisters, Bing Crosby, Chuck Berry, the Rolling Stones, Manhattan Transfer and Depeche Mode.

Chicago's Museum of Science and Industry sponsors a reenactment of the 1895 *Times-Herald* Race and a Glidden Tour for restored cars is held, triggering the interest in antique cars.

Ford and G.M. cancel plans for compact cars, believing that the market will sustain more profitable large cars.

Bitter 113-day strike against G.M. ends, leading to "pattern bargaining"— almost identical contracts between the UAW and the Big Three (Ford, G.M. and Chrysler). Walter Reuther: "I'd rather negotiate with G.M. than the government; G.M. has no army."

First automatic car wash—Detroit.

First fiberglass-bodied car—the Stout 46.

First automobile radio-telephone appears as cab companies begin to dispatch vehicles by radio.

Chevrolet begins to advertise on TV.

Ford accountants estimate accounts payable by weighing bills on a scale.

Ford vice president Donald Frey tells an engineering audience that the automatic transmission developed in the 1930s was the last great innovation needed by automobiles, a sign of Detroit's engineering complacency.

Charles Kettering (G.M.) develops high octane gasoline that allows a doubling of compression ratios.

British Ministry of Transport recommends limited access motorways and urban ring roads.

British auto engineers advise their government not to take over the Volkswagen factory, thinking the Beetle is "too ugly, bizarre, noisy, flimsy."

British workers strike Ford, winning a reduction of the work week from 72 to 45 hours.

British government ends the horsepower tax, hoping that British cars will be more competitive on the export market.

France introduces a horsepower tax.

U.S. Army of Occupation forces Toyota to recognize a union. Toyota sets the Japanese pattern by making sure that it includes both white collar and blue collar workers and bargains at the company, not industry or shop, level.

1947

Hundred millionth motor vehicle produced.

Henry Ford and William C. Durant die. At the time of his death, Durant is the proprietor of a bowling alley.

Los Angeles shuts down coal-burning factories during an air pollution crisis, but the smog does not go away.

Four inventors working on flying cars give up when the Hall car sheers off its wings on roadside trees during an emergency landing on a rural lane.

Kaiser and Frazer launched. Preston Tucker has organized a corporation to produce his visionary rear-engined "Torpedo." He refuses to add seat belts on the recommendation of his marketing specialists.

G.M.'s Kettering engine (5429-cc., overhead valve, V-8) triggers the post-war horsepower competition.

Studebaker produces a Raymond Loewy-designed, tight-skinned, flat-sided car.

Packard offers power windows and power seats.

Ford opens the first car industry automation department.

Taft-Hartley Act, limiting unions, becomes law over Truman's veto.

UAW purges Communist members.

First MG TC arrives in the United States.

Britain's Labour government nationalizes the long distance trucking industry. Newly elected Conservative government will sell it back in 1953.

London bans downtown parking and shuts down the last horse-operated cab in London.

Police strike leads to massive traffic jams in Paris.

Ettore Bugatti's marque dies with him. His son, whom he had groomed to carry on, died in a racing accident in 1939.

Nuremburg Tribunal hangs Volkswagen's wartime medical officer, Korbel, for allowing slave laborers to starve to death.

Munich rejects proposals to redo the street plan of its bombed out downtown to ease auto travel and pedestrian safety. Almost all German cities, except Kassel, follow suit.

Volkswagen surpasses Ford in German sales.

Enzo Ferrari produces the first car bearing his name, the Type 125 Corsa V-12. The car displays a prancing horse emblem borrowed from a friend of Ferrari's, a World War I Italian air force ace killed in combat.

Cisitalia ransoms Ferdinand Porsche, held captive by the French for his wartime collaboration with Hitler, for one million francs, so that he can design their Grand Prix car. The car's failure will bankrupt Cisitalia.

1948

Donora, Pennsylvania, killer smog—19 dead.

Wally Parks edits the first issue of *Hot Rod Magazine*.

William Faulkner writes: "The American really loves nothing but his automobile."

Elvis Presley's family moves to Memphis in a 1937 Plymouth.

Maurice and Richard McDonald open a highly automated hamburger stand, Los Angeles.

Detroit, Pittsburgh and Baltimore build their first municipal parking garages downtown.

Los Angeles voters reject a proposed rapid transit system for tax and image reasons. Downtown merchants fund the pro-transit campaign, suburban mall developers the opposition.

William Harrah (Reno, Nevada) begins his classic car collection.

U.S. Supreme Court prohibits white-only clauses in suburban property deeds.

Harley Earl-designed Cadillac adds nonfunctional air intakes imitating jet planes and introduces the tail fin.

Red Byron's Ford wins the first NASCAR race, at Daytona Beach.

Santa Barbara Acceleration Association opens the first drag racing track at an abandoned air strip.

Dr. Fletcher Woodward publishes a pioneer vehicle safety article in the *Journal of the American Medical Association* calling for cars to be made as crashproof as airplanes. He wants seat belts, a padded dashboard, safety door latches, and energy absorbing bumpers.

Goodrich introduces tubeless tires. Standard in the United States by 1955.

G.M. and the UAW agree to the first pension plans and COLAs (cost of living adjustments).

Assassins attempt to kill Walter and Victor Reuther.

Total European car registration exceeds ten million (one-sixth the U.S. level).

Ford rejects a chance to buy Volkswagen, now the largest German producer. Ford's president describes the Beetle: "not worth a damn."

Ferdinand Porsche starts his car firm.

British troops break a Communist-led strike at Ford of Germany.

Alex Issigonis designs the Morris Minor with torsion bar suspension and rack and pinion steering. Morris prefers to concentrate production on cheaper prewar models that are not exportable.

Incorrectly anticipating nationalization, Austin and Morris pay dividends of 40 percent and 64 percent, rather than modernizing their factories, a costly blunder.

Rover begins to sell Land Rovers—the first successful European four wheel drive vehicle.

Jaguar XK120 debuts, the world's fastest production car at 200 kph.

Lancia offers the first production V-6s.

Michelin patents radial tires.

Citroën begins production of the 2CV, a two-cylinder, air-cooled micro-car. It will sell seven million units in a 40-year production run, third only to the Model T and the VW Beetle.

Honda Motor Company established with capital of $3,300. Soichiro Honda builds his first motorcycle.

After a series of oil spills, the U.S. Coast Guard orders 288 tankers strengthened.

J. Paul Getty acquires the Neutral Zone (between Kuwait and Iraq) oil concession.

Texaco Star Theater with Milton Berle is the first big television hit.

1949

First shopping center mall—Raleigh, North Carolina.

Route 128, Boston, the first suburban beltway, opens.

South of the Border, an amusement park in South Carolina, opens. Its symbol: a 66-meter-high roadside sombrero.

Flannery O'Connor writes about southern fundamentalists in *Wiseblood*: "Nobody with a good car needs to be justified."

Sam and George Barris open their famous Southern California car customizing shop, the beginning a new art genre.

Half the new cars sold in the United States have radios.

First press reports of "chicken" races in Los Angeles. L.A. police compare drag races to cockfights, triggering a "moral panic" in the city.

Insurance companies begin to surcharge adolescent male drivers after the National Safety Council notes their high death rates.

First drag racing nationals at the Bonneville Salt Flats.

First chopper motorcycles (customized with a long fork) appear in California.

American Automobile Association protests against the excessive size and styling emphasis of Detroit firms.

Model B-A moves Ford sales back into second place. Its mushy suspension system sets the standard for U.S. cars.

G.M. introduces lurid paint colors and the notoriously unsafe, gas-guzzling "hard top" cars.

Chrysler introduces optional disc brakes because its new overhead valve V-8 requires additional braking power. U.S. manufacturers refuse to make them standard for another 30 years.

First turnkey starter introduced by Chrysler.

Atlanta motorist runs over the novelist Margaret Mitchell while she is crossing a street.

U.N. conference sets universal traffic signals.

Colin Chapman founds Lotus.

U.K. Special Roads Act allows limitation of access. In inflation-corrected pounds, Britain is spending less money on roads than in 1911.

Swedish airplane manufacturer, Saab, begins to make cars.

Ferrari begins to export cars to the United States.

Ferrucio Lamborghini starts a tractor firm.

Isuzu begins to produce British Hillmans.

Gen. Douglas MacArthur, the U.S. viceroy in Japan, leads a purge of Communists in Japanese unions.

Japanese government creates the Ministry of International Trade and Industry, which will mastermind the Japanese industrial boom.

Total African motor vehicle registration exceeds a million.

U.S. oil production declines for the first time. Middle Eastern and Venezuelan oil is cheaper.

1950

California biochemist Aarlie Hagen-Smit demonstrates the relationship between auto emissions and smog.

William Levitt builds Levittown, Pennyslvania, typical postwar auto-dependent suburb.

Nearly half the Americans under age 30 answering the Kinsey survey acknowledge having had premarital sex in autos.

Ford's new F-100 pickup ("Where men are men, trucks are Ford V-8s") starts the trend to more stylish pickups sold as status objects, not just load carriers.

Harry Truman replaces a Lincoln with a Cadillac as the presidential car.

Jack Benny's TV show debuts—signature car a 1929 Maxwell.

One-year-old Bruce Springsteen's family moves into the top floor of a three decker next to Ducky Slattery's Sinclair Station, which sparks his boyhood ambition to become a mechanic.

Auto accidents surpass tuberculosis to become fourth leading killer in the United States.

First NASCAR superspeedway opens at Darlington, South Carolina.

Bill Kenz and Roy Leslie build the first twin engine dragster, the 777. Treads rip from the tires when raced.

U.S. auto insurance losses pass $1 billion.

G.M. appoints its first safety engineer, a former race car driver named Howard Gandelot. He, like most race drivers, opposes seat belts, because he believes that they encourage dangerous driving by giving a false illusion of safety.

UAW-G.M. "Treaty of Detroit" ushers in an era of industry-union cooperation.

The United States produces 79.4 percent of world's cars.

Governor Frank Driscoll opens the New Jersey Turnpike, announcing: "Motorists can now see the beauty of the real New Jersey." Travel time from New York to Philadelphia reduced from five to two hours.

Motorists are fewer than 5 percent of commuters entering the City of London.

Rover Whizzard, prototype turbine car, averages less than 5 mpg (2.1 kpl).

Britain ends gasoline rationing, in place since 1939.

Britain exports 60 percent of its car production, an all-time high.

West German government returns 30 percent control of Daimler-Benz to Friedrich Frick. The Allied War Crimes Commission had confiscated it because he had helped the Nazis loot Jewish firms in the 1930s and had used slave labor in the 1940s.

U.S. engineer Edwards Deming lectures in Japan on quality control.

Toyota ends a major strike, fires union activists.

Eiji Toyoda visits River Rouge Ford plant.

Japan still derives more energy from firewood than oil.

Three major refineries are built in Western Europe to process Middle Eastern oil.

Saudis get a "50%-50%" deal from Aramco.

1951

Bulletin of Atomic Scientists favors decentralized cities for civil defense.

Hundred millionth U.S.-built car takes to the road.

Herman Dengel runs over Elma Wischmeir in Cleveland, Ohio, the one millionth U.S. traffic fatality.

Ford ad: "The American road is paved with hope."

Some San Franciscans unsuccessfully oppose the city's new freeway plan.

Jackie Brenston and the Kings of Rhythm (including young Ike Turner) sing "Rocket 88" (after an Oldsmobile muscle car), credited as the first rock and roll song by Sam Phillips, Little Richard and Bill Haley.

TV show "Amos 'n Andy" perpetuates the racist stereotype of the Cadillac-owning, shiftless black in its character, Kingfish.

Roy Rogers' TV show: signature car, a stubborn Jeep named "Nellybelle."

Hot Rod Magazine editor Wally Parks founds the National Hot Rod Association. Within two years, 15,000 rodders will join.

Chrysler offers hemispherical-type ("hemi-head") combustion chamber engine, power brakes and power steering.

Buick offers the first tinted windshields. Safety experts complain that they reduce night vision by 15 percent.

Air bag patented in the United States.

New York's Museum of Modern Art recognizes the Italian car design firm Pininfarina for its Fiat-powered 1946 Cisitalia and Ford designer John Tjaarda for the streamlined 1934 Mercury Zephyr.

Picasso sculpture, *Baboon and Young*, features an ape with a head shaped like a Renault.

Britain introduces lined ("zebra") street crossings, where pedestrians have the right of way.

Soviets begin a failed attempt to market Moskvitch cars, made with looted Opel tools, in Western Europe. They advise customers to see Opel dealers for spare parts.

Iranian prime minister Mossadegh nationalizes the British oil concession.

1952

First Holiday Inn opened—Memphis, Tennessee.

For the first time motorists register more cars in Los Angeles than New York City.

California ends Pacific Electric trolley service in the median strip of the Hollywood Freeway, ending hopes for a rail/freeway system.

Disney cartoon, *Susie, the Little Blue Coupe*, has an anthropomorphic car.

Top drag racers exceed 288 kph, up from 208 in 1948 and 160 in 1939. They are no longer "street legal," burning nitromethane and driven by professional drivers.

Business Week notes that hot rodders spend $50 million a year on parts.

Lincoln is the first U.S. make to spend $100 per car in advertising.

Gordon Buehrig-designed all metal Ford Ranchwagon breaks with the "woody" look for station wagons. Within three years, station wagon sales will triple, accounting for 10 percent of the U.S. market.

Hoping to regain the number one spot from Chevrolet, Ford begins a price war that will lead to the Hudson, Nash and Packard bankruptcies.

Ford begins to plan its new Edsel division, designed to move into the midrange market controlled by G.M. Poet Marianne Moore suggests "Resilient Bullet" and "Utopian Turtle" as names.

Chrysler introduces hydraulic shock absorbers.

Safety expert Hugh DeHaven presents the results of a crash data survey done by the Indiana State Police, which showed that 80 percent of car crashes knocked car doors open, accounting for 46 percent of driver fatalities. By 1955 the Big Three have all adopted interlocking door latches. One Indiana state trooper coins the phrase "second collision" to describe the impact within a car after a crash.

Last trolley (tram) in London.

London killer smog: 4,000 dead.

Germany ends speed limits on the autobahns. Frankfurt adopts staggered traffic lights, 30 years after they became commonplace in the United States.

Blaupunkt (West Germany) develops push button FM car radios.

Mercedes introduces the 300SL with gull wing doors, the first production fuel injection car.

Ferdinand Porsche dies.

Austin and Morris merge to form British Motors Corporation (B.M.C.). The new firm continues to underinvest in plant improvements, spending one-third less than Ford of Great Britain.

Berliet family regains control of its truck firm, operated by a workers' cooperative since the end of the war.

Moscow Beltway, first limited access road in the USSR.

Ford attempts to buy into Toyota fail.

Suzuki Loom Works produces its first motorcycle, three years before its first car.

1953

New York killer smog: 200 dead.

Largest entirely white community in the United States is Levittown, Long Island, the quintessential auto age suburb. Most of its 70,000 residents hold federally guaranteed mortgages.

Automobile Manufacturer's Association begins to lobby against urban toll roads, believing that freeways will generate more traffic and sales, especially in "under-automobiled" cities like New York.

Philadelphia (Schuykill Expressway), Detroit (John Lodge Expressway) and Pittsburgh (Penn-Lincoln Parkway) build their first freeways from downtown to the suburbs.

Marlon Brando makes his film debut in *The Wild One*, the first motorcycle gang movie.

Country and western singer Hank Williams dies in a pickup truck accident.

Forty-one antique car collections open to the public or museums exist in the United States.

More eight-cylinder than six-cylinder cars sold in the United States.

Chrysler reduces car weight by 600 pounds, loses market share to Ford as a result. The American public adores big and heavy.

Kaiser-Frazer buys Willys-Overland.

Buick engineers tell the Society of Automotive Engineers how they redesigned their engine to fit the space allowed by stylists, a sign that styling has triumphed over engineering in Detroit.

Innovations: first 12-volt electrical system appears on G.M. cars. Within three years it is the industry standard. Idiot lights begin to replace gauges in U.S. cars. Chevrolet introduces the Corvette, the first plastic-bodied car made in quantity.

U.S. Air Force, worried about losing personnel in car accidents, orders its crash experts to test cars. After five years, Congress ends funding because of pressure from Detroit.

Mack introduces its Thermodyne diesel engine, which will make massive semis and articulated trucks possible.

Volkswagen opens a Brazilian subsidiary. One year later it also moves into Mexico.

Genevieve, a British car-racing film, features a 1905 Darracq in the title role.

Merchants on the Lijnbaan, a street where Rotterdam has banned traffic, report a business upsurge.

After a 100-day strike, Nissan breaks its independent union.

Shah of Iran, with CIA help, overthrows the socialist prime minister, Mossadegh. The shah does not return control of Iranian oil to British Petroleum, but turns it over to an American-dominated consortium.

1954

Ray Kroc buys out the McDonald brothers.

Victor Gruen designs Northland Center (Detroit), the first mall with landscaped internal pedestrian walkways.

Rev. Robert Schuller opens a drive-in church, Garden Grove, California. Schuller describes it as "a shopping center for Jesus Christ."

Rumors spread throughout Seattle that fallout from recent H-bomb tests is pitting car windshields.

New York highway czar Robert Moses: "When you operate in an overbuilt metropolis, you have to hack your way with a meat ax."

Dinah Shore sings "See the U.S.A. in your Chevrolet."

Height of the New York City doo-wop craze. Ghetto groups choose such car names as Edsels, Cadillacs, Fleetwoods, Impalas, Fiestas and Belvederes.

Daytona calls out the National Guard to stop 10,000 rioting drag racers, arresting 85. Los Angeles police arrest 125 dragsters at a street race.

Hot Rod Magazine issues two records by Leadfoot Darensbourg and His Flatout Five, featuring "authentic race and garage sounds."

U.S. military begins to sponsor drag-racing teams and to advertise for mechanics in *Hot Rod Magazine*.

AETNA Insurance underwrites the National Hot Rod Association, giving it enormous power.

New York parking lot firms complain that wider, longer 1950s cars have shrunk the number of parking spots in Manhattan by 15 percent.

General Foods moves its headquarters from Manhattan to the suburbs.

Cornell University lab studies, financed by Liberty Mutual Insurance, prove the advantages of auto seat belts.

As traffic fatalities soar in the United States, New York City's traffic commissioner notes that most drivers "are not sufficiently trained, nor physically able to handle the horsepower placed at their disposal." Detroit has not improved brakes enough to handle the increased weight and speed of 1950s cars.

After pressure from the National Safety Council and state motor vehicle agencies, the Big Three promise to abandon racing and the horsepower race.

Breathalyzer invented.

Cadillac introduces a vision-distorting wraparound windshield made by Libby-Owens-Ford. For the first time, most cars sold in the United States have automatic transmissions.

Greyhound introduces the glass-domed bus.

Richard Berg bicycles from Santa Monica to New York City in 14 days.

Vietnamese invent freight bicycles (500-lb. capacity) to supply their troops at Dien Bien Phu, where they destroy the French army.

Volkswagen becomes the fourth largest car manufacturer in the world. The German government privatizes the firm.

German engineer Felix Wankel develops a rotary internal combustion engine.

British Parliament allows American-style parking meters, if towns earmark the fees for downtown parking garages. London installs the first ones outside the U.S. Embassy in 1958.

Ford sells its French factory to Simca.

The United States becomes a net oil importer for first time.

1955

American families spend more money on auto transportation than on housing or clothing.

James Dean sets the prototype for alienated drag-racing adolescents in the film *Rebel without a Cause*. Dean later dies in an accident in his 1954 Porsche Spyder.

Elvis Presley paints his first Cadillac black and pink. According to one Elvis biographer, Cadillacs were his favorite "nontoxic recreation."

Buddy Holly chauffeurs Elvis Presley, in Lubbock, Texas, for a concert, around town, decides to become a rock singer also.

Chuck Berry's commercial rock and roll hit "Maybelline" develops the car seduction theme. He also celebrates 1950s car marketing with "No Money Down."

Hot Rod Magazine, now claiming a readership of more than one million, says that sports cars are "hot rods in disguise."

Vladimir Nabokov's hero, Humbert Humbert, comments about the American roadside after a long, pederastic trip with Lolita: "We had been everywhere, we had seen nothing." He notes, "Nothing is more exciting than Philistine vulgarity."

Ralph Nader graduates from Harvard Law School after writing a major paper on auto design and product liability.

Peak of Big Three hegemony in the United States: G.M. controls 50 percent of the market, Ford 27 percent, and Chrysler 17 percent. The oligopoly's profits are nearly double those of other U.S. industrial firms. Together they control two-thirds of the world market. The remaining U.S. firms, Studebaker (recent purchaser of Packard) and American Motors (formed by the recent merger of Nash and Kelvinator) control tiny market shares. Despite $150 million in capital investment, Kaiser fails.

G.M. makes over one billion dollars, the highest income ever earned by a corporation.

Designer Raymond Loewy complains that the tail-finned, overchromed, 1950s car is "a jukebox on wheels."

Pontiac introduces two-tone cars.

Twelve top-selling U.S. car models have double the horsepower of their predecessors.

Detroit manufacturers decide to get out of racing and not to introduce emissions controls on cars, unless all three companies agree.

More than 10 million trucks registered in United States.

VW introduces the Beetle in the United States. Within three years it sells 50,000 units.

At least 20 German cities have at least one traffic-free street.

Enough Londoners own cars to allow business as usual during a transit strike.

Capetown (South Africa)-North Cape (Norway) trip takes 86 days.

French film, *Wages of Fear*, is the first European trucking movie.

Rear-engined Renault Dauphine debuts; will sell one million models.

Renault president Lafeucheux killed in a car crash.

Worst racing disaster, at LeMans: 82 killed.

Alberto Ascari becomes the first race driver to crash into Monaco harbor.

Japan's Ministry of International Trade and Industry targets the auto industry for protection (high tariff) and development (capital infusion).

Thirteen U.S. service station chains begin to offer premium gasoline.

Soviets export three million tons of oil to Western Europe.

Admiral Lewis Strauss, U.S. Navy, predicts that by the 1970s nuclear energy costs will be so cheap that electricity will be unmetered.

1956

Car pools enable Montgomery, Alabama, blacks to boycott successfully the local bus company, beginning the modern civil rights movement.

Los Angeles Police Department buys a Hillier 12c helicopter to report on traffic for radio stations.

Victor Gruen designs Southdale Center (Minneapolis), the first mall with an enclosed, climate-controlled pedestrian court.

"Classic" film *Hot Rod Girl* advertises: "It's good girls gone bad again, as four teens steal cars, selling them to a junk yard dealer to make money. When one of the girls kills a motorcycle cop during a chicken race, the trouble really begins."

Solid Gold Cadillac depicts the car as the ultimate cinematic symbol of wealth.

Elizabeth Taylor saves actor Montgomery Clift's life by crawling into his car and pulling his front teeth out of his throat after he drives into a telephone pole.

Cincinnati used car dealer offers to break 50 Elvis Presley records for each car he sells.

Chrysler offers an in-car record player.

Famous painter Jackson Pollock dies in a car crash.

Shirley Roque drops out of high school, marries gas station attendant Jack Muldowney, and begins to drag race a 1940 Ford with a Cadillac engine on rural highways near Schenectady, New York.

Danny Eames and Chuck Daigh drive from New York to Los Angeles in a record and highly illegal 47 hours.

U.S. intercity airline traffic surpasses bus traffic.

New York-Chicago toll road/turnpike system complete.

National Defense and Interstate Highway Act passed. President Eisenhower argues: "In case of atomic attack on our cities, the road net must allow quick evacuation of target areas."

U.S. Congress limits manufacturer control of dealers.

U.S. Supreme Court rules that Detroit must sell to discount dealers.

Ford stock goes on the market, ending the largest family-owned business in the world.

Ford offers seat belts for the first time. It blames declining sales on unconscious consumer resistance to the new technology.

Chrysler introduces "Torqueflite" three-speed automatic transmission and the dangerous push button transmission.

"Safety" door locks standard on U.S. cars. Packard introduces electric locks. G.M. standardizes dashboard control locations.

Alfred P. Sloan retires as G.M. chairman of the board.

Only one American car, Studebaker, averages better than 8 kpl at 100 kph.

German auto production surpasses Britain's, is now the second largest in the world. German cars are the most fuel efficient.

Great Britain has 4,000 traffic lights, fewer than New York City.

BMW introduces the Isetta, a notoriously unsafe front entry, rear-engined bubble car.

Fuji Heavy Industries starts its subsidiary, Subaru, to make mopeds.

After the first Arab oil boycott, broken by U.S. and Russian exports, European car makers seek to increase fuel economy. This search ultimately leads to front wheel drive cars.

Occidental Petroleum breaks the Aramco monopoly on Arab oil by signing contract with Libya. Oil found in Nigeria and Algeria.

1957

Jack Kerouac's novel, *On the Road*, popularizes the Odyssey theme in modern novels.

In James Agee's novel, *A Death in the Family*, a fatal car accident shatters a small town family.

"Leave It To Beaver" television show begins—signature car, a 1956 Chevrolet station wagon.

Former marine pilot Max Schumacher begins helicopter traffic reports for KMPC, Los Angeles.

Architect Stanley Meston designs the first arches for McDonald's.

Sixty-six-year-old gas station operator Harlan Sanders, facing bankruptcy because the interstate has bypassed him, decides to franchise his Kentucky Fried Chicken restaurant.

Charles Wilson, secretary of defense and former president of G.M., tells Congress: "What was good for our country was good for General Motors and *vice versa*."

Chevy 265-cubic-inch V-8 delivers one horsepower per cubic inch.

Chrysler adopts torsion bar suspension.

G.M. offers 75 body styles and 450 trim combinations.

Dupont divests its G.M. stock after an antitrust suit.

New rear engine Fiat 500, which will sell 1.5 million units, introduced.

Japan becomes the world's leading steel producer.

Toyota becomes the first car maker to allow individual workers to stop the assembly line if they spot a defect. Its head production engineer, Taiichi Ohno, improves die change time from 24 hours to 3 minutes.

Japan's Arabian Oil Company gets the Neutral Zone offshore concession.

1958

Hollywood begins to glamorize "good old boy" moonshiner types in the film *Thunder Road*.

John Keats publishes *Insolent Chariots* and Colin Buchanan publishes *Mixed Blessings: The Motor Car in Britain*, harbingers of the anti-auto literature of the 1960s.

Auto-industry-financed "safety establishment" tells U.S. House auto safety hearings that education, not vehicle engineering, is the way to improve safety.

TV show "77 Sunset Strip" features a Thunderbird convertible as a signature car for Ed Byrnes.

Peak year for drive-in movie theaters—4,063.

Hot Rod Magazine, impressed by the huge new 1950s engines, reluctantly acknowledges that "real" hot rods can adopt other engines beside the V-8s that Ford has made since 1932.

Over $1 billion in federal funds spent on urban freeways.

Los Angeles survey shows that the Harbor, Hollywood and San Bernardino freeways have exceeded capacity within four years of construction.

New York City closes the extension of Fifth Avenue through Washington Square.

New York Central Railroad begins to offer truck "piggyback" service.

S. I. Hayakawa, later a conservative Republican senator from California, attacks the Big Three for their "assault on consumer intelligence."

Air suspension standard on U.S. cars.

Ford introduces the Edsel, a massive failure. Consumers do not like its "horse collar" grille, poor reliability or dangerous push button electronic transmission.

In a recession year, compact Nash Ramblers enjoy a vogue and U.S. auto imports (mostly Volkswagens) exceed exports for the first time since 1890s, control 8 percent of market. Buick dealers begin to sell the Opel Kadett, first imported car sold by a Big Three firm.

Henry Ford II describes the Beetle as a "little shit box."

Road and Track describes the first Japanese export to the United States, an underpowered Datsun, as having a "melancholy" performance.

William Mitchell replaces Harley Earl as G.M.'s chief stylist. He will drop tail fins and reduce chrome for the "London-tailored" look. Still, Buick sets record—58 pounds of chrome trim—and Mitchell's 1959 Cadillac will have 107-centimeter tail fins, the biggest ever.

Production of Packard cars stops.

Ford and G.M. end experiments with air bags, refuse to share data with others, after Congress authorizes an antitrust exemption for safety research. The new Safety Compact does not have a single employee for seven years and enacts only one "safety standard," a ban on radial tires.

Ford announces a program to develop a nuclear-powered car, the Nucleon.

G.M., hoping to increase engine power further, seeks permission from the U.S. Public Health Service to add more lead to gasoline.

Dupont patents polypropylene plastics.

Monroney Act requires price stickers on cars, seeks to limit high pressure sales tactics.

World motor vehicle registration exceeds 100 million (70% in the United States). Moscow, Idaho, has more gas stations than Moscow, USSR.

First British motorway opens.

First CVT (continuously variable transmission) introduced on the DAF Daffodil.

East Germany begins to make its answer to the VW Beetle, the Trabant, which features an underpowered two-stroke engine and plastic body. The car, which produces nine times the hydrocarbons of Western cars, remains in production until unification in 1990.

Datsun (Nissan) wins a 16,000-kilometer Australian rally—first overseas racing victory for a Japanese car.

For the first time, the Japanese auto industry relies only on Japanese components.

First Japanese overseas factory—Toyota of Brazil.

Subaru builds its first car, designed by the same engineers who built the Zero fighter plane.

Recently elected leftist government in Venezuela backs away from plans to nationalize oil, astutely fearing a U.S.-sponsored coup.

ENI, the Italian national oil company, already a large purchaser of Soviet oil, further undercuts the major oil companies by offering royalties of 75 percent of profits to Middle Eastern countries.

1959

Morris Mini Minor (designed by British engineer Alex Issigonis) begins the modern generation of front wheel drive cars with transversely mounted engines. B.M.C. goes bankrupt before it can produce the new design effectively. By 1986 five million Mini Minors have been sold, the fourth best of any model.

Sociologist Vance Packard notes: "The primary function of the motor car in America is to carry its owner into a higher social stratum."

Folklorists find numerous local versions of the "prosthetic hook in the car handle" lover's lane story popular with adolescents all over the United States.

Lee Petty wins the first 800-kilometer race at the Daytona International Speedway.

Indianapolis 800 requires fire retardant uniforms for drivers.

Cadillac introduces cruise control.

Central Artery, Boston, completed at a cost of $65.6 million per kilometer, believed to be the most expensive road ever built.

Five-year-old Bay Shore Freeway has the worst traffic jams in Los Angeles.

Swiss photographer Robert Frank publishes a famous collection, *The Americans*, which emphasizes the roadside strip as the center of American culture.

Stockholm creates the first bus-only lanes.

Japan begins motorway construction.

Earle MacPherson's struts first appear on a British Ford.

Rolls-Royce imitates Detroit, adopts a V-8 engine.

Bavaria buys BMW to avoid a British takeover.

Brazil decides to emphasize roads, not railroads, in developing its interior.

President Eisenhower imposes an oil import quota of 15 percent. The quota will protect domestic producers whose oil is too expensive to compete in world markets until Nixon revokes it in 1973.

Arab Petroleum Congress meets in Cairo. Occidental strikes oil in Libya. These are precursors of the energy crisis since the other Arab producers are envious of the high price that Occidental pays Libya.

Dutch natural gas fields (largest outside Soviet Union) discovered.

1960

U.S. Public Health Survey begins an urban air-monitoring program.

The United States has 3,841 shopping centers, 19 with a floor area over one million square feet.

New York City rejects a $57 million proposal to add 10,000 more downtown parking spaces and hires the first meter maids.

New York State bans driving for "sexual perverts" and "those advocating the violent overthrow of the government." Illinois denies licenses to rapists, pederasts, homosexuals and prostitutes.

Twelve million U.S. children (38% of the total) ride school buses.

Drag racers riot in San Diego.

Beginnings of the dune buggy craze.

TV show, "Route 66," set on that road, features a Corvette wrecked in each year's final episode.

George Barris gold plates Elvis's Cadillac and customizes it with white fur seats, television, telephone, record player, bar, ice maker and an electric shoe buffer.

Denver cement truck driver Robert O. Porter fills a friend's convertible with concrete. Within a year folklore with local details appears across the United States, usually involving a husband filling his wife's lover's Cadillac. By 1973 localized versions have appeared in Bergen, Norway, and Nairobi, Kenya.

Jack Brabham brings a mid-engined Cooper to Indianapolis, starting a new trend that dooms the traditional Indy roadster.

Big Three repel the Volkswagen invasion by introducing compact cars: Corvair, Falcon and Valiant.

Revolutionary (flat six, rear engine, air-cooled), but dangerous, Chevrolet Corvair debuts. Accountants eliminate the torsion bar suspension from the Corvair, guaranteeing some rollover accidents while cornering. *Consumer's*

Reports warns its readers of the defects. *Motor Trend* names it car of the year.

Chrysler introduces the alternator and flasher light.

Chrysler ends the DeSoto line.

Transatlantic ships begin to offer piggyback service.

Skid mark left by a Jaguar in an English accident measures 285 meters.

Britain increases the speed limit to 40 mph (64 kph).

B.M.C. purchases Jaguar.

French novelist Albert Camus killed in a car accident.

Stockholm police complain of Swedish adolescent hot rodders—the *Raggare*: "Their cars have become their God."

On a visit to the United States, Soviet premier Nikita Khrushchev asks about tail fins: "What do those things do anyway?" Shortly thereafter, tail fins will appear on Soviet-made Zil limousines.

Honda begins to market cars with four valves per cylinder.

First Toyota exported to the United States.

Organization of Petroleum Exporting Countries (OPEC) formed.

India forces oil companies to drop prices by threatening to buy Soviet oil.

Japanese oil consumption doubles 1957 levels, now equals coal consumption.

1961

Ratio of highway fatalities to motor vehicles: Italy, 1:375; West Germany, 1:430; Japan, 1:526; France, 1:935; United Kingdom, 1:1,410; United States, 1:2,000.

Traffic fatalities per 100,000 population in the United States are 22.1. For divorced males in their 20s, the rate is ten times higher.

Federal government begins to cross-list names of those receiving traffic tickets for the states.

G.M., despite having the worst safety record in the industry, refuses to adopt padded dashboards, opts instead for what its safety engineers call a "meat cleaver" dash because stylists favor it.

Last interurban trolley line in Los Angeles abandoned. Santa Monica Freeway finally reaches the San Fernando Valley.

Chicago estimates that it has spent $350 million on street widening since 1910 in a failed attempt to retrofit its street system to the automobile, the equivalent of what two new subway lines would cost.

Phil Hill becomes the first American world champion driver.

William Faulkner's *The Town* describes the arrival of the first cars in small town Mississippi. The principal character's red sports car is "invincibly and irrevocably polygamous."

Priest/novelist/sociologist Andrew Greeley writes about "the cult of the sacred car."

Walt Disney discovers cars in *The Absent Minded Professor*. A Model T Ford is the first car with super powers.

First U.S. V-6 offered by Buick.

Ford's new E-Coat paint process becomes the world standard. Ford does not fully adopt it until 1984.

Ford buys the radio manufacturer, Philco.

Lee Iacocca kills the Ford Cardinal, a projected front wheel drive car.

Successful assassins, armed with CIA-provided weapons, riddle Dominican dictator Rafael Trujillo's turquoise and gray 1956 Chevrolet sedan with more than 50 shots.

Honda becomes the dominant motorcycle manufacturer in world.

Isuzu begins to design and build its own cars.

West German firm makes Amphicars, the only production amphibious cars ever sold. They leak and cost more than buying a car, motorboat and trailer separately.

"The Avengers" appears on British TV with John Steed driving a 1930s Rolls-Royce, Emma Peel a Lotus Elan and Tara King a Lotus Esprit. Peel and King are the first woman TV stars with signature cars.

British troops frustrate a planned Iraqi takeover of Kuwait.

1962

Life magazine writes: "In California, the car is like an extra, highly essential part of the human anatomy."

For the first time Southern California builders construct more apartments than single family homes, a sign that space is becoming short.

San Francisco rejects an expressway, beginning the urban antihighway revolt.

Copenhagen closes its main shopping street, the Strøget, to traffic.

Cincinnati's Bureau of Air Pollution notes that smoke pollution has declined 90 percent since 1947, but car-based pollution (800 tons a year) is up 111 percent.

U.S. intercity bus traffic surpasses that of railroads.

French conceptual artist Arman blows up an MG, entitles the shattered remains *White Orchid*, and shows them in a museum.

William Faulkner's *The Reivers* focuses on learning to drive as *the* initiation rite into adulthood.

Edward Ruscha, *Twenty-six Gasoline Stations*, first photo essay on roadside architecture, features U.S. Route 66.

American governments spend $10 billion on highways.

U.S. Supreme Court's *Baker v. Carr* decision (one person—one vote) promises to lessen rural domination of state highway planning.

Firsts: transistorized ignition systems, by Pontiac; and turbocharged production car, a Chevrolet Corvair Monza Spyder.

Ford ends production of the V-8 engine introduced in 1932.

For the Civil War centennial Chrysler sells a "Dixie Special" Valiant, available only in "Confederate Gray."

Webb Pierce's tastefully customized Bonneville Cadillac includes a thousand silver dollars woven into the fetal calfskin upholstery. The hood sports ornamental rifles.

Anne Ford's (Henry II's daughter) debut costs $250,000.

Volkswagen becomes the first European firm to produce one million cars in a year.

German writer W. Forst: "Sixteen years after the end of the war our cities are again without wounds; they appear to be booming, but they are threatened by chaos. Like locusts eating the fields, so do cars take possession of our streets and squares."

Traffic speeds in London are the lowest ever recorded. Private cars occupy 47 percent of the street space during rush hours, but carry only 10 percent of the travelers.

James Bond's signature car, an Aston-Martin, appears in *Dr. No.*

Shelby begins producing the Cobra.

Kennedy round of tariff negotiations under the General Agreement on Trade and Tariffs (GATT) leads to a reduction of about 50 percent in tariffs on cars for Western Europe and the United States.

Chain gear Honda S500, first Japanese sports car.

Nigeria begins to export oil.

1963

President John F. Kennedy assassinated in his open 1961 Lincoln Continental limousine, leading to the development of bulletproof, bubble-top limousines.

Amos Burke is the first U.S. TV detective with a foreign car—a Rolls-Royce. "Beverly Hillbillies" is the top-ranked show on TV—signature car, a 1930s pickup truck.

Joe Flower's 1956 Chevrolet, *Venus*, wins the first Autorama car-customizing show. Many cars displayed are immobile.

"Car stolen with dead grandmother in tarpaulin on roof" folklore story spreads across the United States from San Jose, California. European versions crop up within two years.

"Drag City": most successful of the drag-racing rock and roll songs.

Downtown Boston gridlocks as 100,000 cars search for 37,000 downtown spaces until 9 P.M.

Boston's Route 128, only 15 years old, is doubled in width.

San Francisco carbon monoxide levels for the year exceed seven parts per million, an all-time high, three times 1984 levels.

California requires positive crankcase ventilation systems to reduce hydrocarbon emissions. All U.S. manufacturers adopt the system for all cars.

Parnelli Jones, first driver to break 150 mph (240 kph) at Indy.

Studebaker halts car production in the United States.

Major adoption of one way streets in London increases volume 10 percent, reduces travel time 20 percent, and reduces accidents 20 percent.

Influential British governmental report *Traffic in Towns* (the *Buchanan Report*) recommends much more pedestrian protection, especially price rationing for downtown traffic entry. The report sparks a bitter debate between urban planners and traffic engineers.

British Rover markets a "safety" car.

Mercedes-Benz reenters the U.S. market.

1964

Lewis Mumford writes in *The Highway and the City* that the auto is "a compensatory device for enlarging an ego which had been shrunken by our very success in mechanization."

Edward Keinholz's graphic sculpture, *Back Seat Dodge-'38*, which depicts passionless, mechanical backseat sex, attracts over 70,000 viewers. Museum censors finally close the back door of the car.

Liquor implicated in about half of U.S. traffic fatalities.

Harlan "Colonel" Sanders sells the largest roadside fast food chain (600 outlets) in the United States to John Y. Brown for $2 million. Seven years later Brown sells the chain for $275 million to Heublin.

Prominent architectural critic Peter Blake publishes *God's Own Junkyard*, an attack on roadside schlock. He especially attacks the duck-shaped restaurant in Riverhead Long Island.

U.S. auto companies make lap belts available.

Corvair, Falcon and Valiant sales reduce imports to less than 5 percent of the U.S. market.

Corvair gets a $15 stabilizing bar, the key to reducing its dangerous death rate, but only because Chevrolet vice president Bunky Knudsen threatens to resign after his niece dies in a preventable Corvair roll-over accident.

G.M. becomes the first U.S. auto company to hire women designers.

G.M. vice president John DeLorean introduces the Pontiac Tempest (later grandiloquently renamed after the Ferrari GTO), first of the low-priced 1960s muscle cars (6371-cc., V-8 engine). It sells 38,000 units, although DeLorean said it "rattled . . . like it was carrying rocks" and *Road Test Magazine* said it "was the worst riding and handling car available."

Plymouth advertises its muscle car's hemi engine: "You can't make an engine like this with figures and formulas only. . . . It's got to be voodoo, baby!"

Chrysler offers the first five-year, 50,000-mile (80,000 km) warranty.

Automatic transmission selection pattern standardized.

Santa Monica Freeway completed, essentially finishing Los Angeles's freeway system.

Verrazano-Narrows Bridge, New York City: 1,298 meters.

Japan's fatality *rate* per car has declined 64 percent since 1964, but the number of deaths is up 20 percent.

Scooter-riding Mods and motorcycle-riding Rockers riot in Britain.

Grand St. Bernard Tunnel, Switzerland-Italy: 5.84 kilometers.

First Wankel rotary-engined car, NSU Sport Prinz.

Lamborghini, the tractor manufacturer, begins to make sports cars.

DeGaulle prohibits Ford from reentering France as a manufacturer.

Exxon's worldwide slogan: "Put a tiger in your tank."

6

End of the Honeymoon: 1965–1980

1965

Nader, *Unsafe at Any Speed*, and O'Connell and Myers, *Safety Last*, launch muckraking attacks on the auto industry.

Ribicoff Committee claims that Detroit manufacturing quality has declined to the point that car makers have recalled 20 percent of the cars made in the 1960s.

Auto fatality rates are up 15 percent since 1960, reversing a 37 percent decline since 1947.

Wall Street Journal criticizes G.M. for spending less than one-tenth of one percent (0.1%) of its annual budget on safety.

Peak year for hydrocarbon and carbon monoxide emissions in the Los Angeles Basin.

Motor Vehicle Air Pollution Control Act passed.

Highway Beautification Act seeks to limit billboards in the United States.

Lower Manhattan Expressway canceled after sit-in by neighborhood activists, led by Jane Jacobs.

Bloody riots in the Watts, Los Angeles, ghetto include a handmade sign in the middle of a through street used by white suburban commuters: "Turn left or get shot."

Berry Gordy claims that he imitates Ford assembly line techniques to turn out stylish Motown singing groups.

Lee Iacocca places a 4261-cc. V-8 engine in the compact Falcon, renames the beautifully styled car the Mustang.

Detroit sells a half-million convertibles, the peak.

G.M. settles a nine-year-old antitrust suit over its 85 percent control of the bus market.

On approximately this date, the Indiana State Police adopt radar to measure speeds.

Los Angeles Police Department issues 2,000 citations for road racing.

National Hot Rod Association licenses Shirley Muldowney, the first woman allowed to operate a top fuel dragster.

"My Mother, the Car," arguably the worst TV sit-com ever, debuts—first anthropomorphic auto on TV (voice by Ann Southern). "Get Smart" is the top-rated TV show—signature car, a Fiat Spider. Honey West and Ironside—first TV detectives with vans.

"Tombstone Every Mile" is first trucking song to top the country and western music charts.

Tom Wolfe's *Kandy*Kolored*Tangerine Flaked Streamlined Baby* adulates the Southern California adolescent car-customizing culture.

Ken Kesey and his Merry Pranksters take their psychedelic-colored bus cross-country to hype L.S.D.

Highest speed ever attained by a wheel-driven car, 776 kph, by Bob Summers's Goldenrod Streamliner at the Bonneville Salt Flats, Utah.

Mobile home sales pass 200,000 per year.

Mt. Blanc Tunnel, Switzerland-Italy—12.1 kilometers.

Britain finally adopts the continental symbolic signs.

Rolls-Royce is the last auto firm to adopt integral frame construction.

Volkswagen buys Audi (formerly Auto-Union), hoping to upsize its cars as Beetle sales lag. Evidently Germans no longer want "a car for people who wish to distinguish themselves from people who wish to distinguish themselves."

Germany begins a new wave of autobahn construction, with the New York State Thruway as a model.

Citroën purchases Panhard and liquidates it.

William Levitt begins to build American-style tract houses outside Paris, an exercise in cultural imperialism that will bankrupt him.

Toyota Corona—first Japanese car really suited to U.S. conditions.

Toyota sells its one millionth Corolla, the first Japanese model to reach that level.

Tokyo abandons its greenbelt parks for suburban housing.

First Grand Prix victory by a Japanese car—Honda at Mexico.

Premier Alexei Kosygin calls for a great expansion of Soviet car production in the next five-year plan.

Worst motor vehicle accident ever—two trucks plow into a crowd in Sotoboua, Togo, killing 125.

1966

Widely publicized Muskie Committee hearings generate public interest in air pollution, especially auto emissions.

National Transportation and Motor Vehicle Safety Act becomes law.

Big Three firms, under government pressure, offer collapsible steering wheels.

In *Schmerber v. California*, the U.S. Supreme Court rules that police may take blood for alcohol testing from arrested drivers without their consent.

Of the 146 million tons of pollutants in the U.S. atmosphere, 86 million tons come from cars.

George Barris builds TV's Batmobile, a customized Ford V-8, for $75,000.

"Green Hornet" TV show: signature car, a souped up Chrysler Imperial.

Pioneer traffic reporter Max Schumacher dies in a helicopter crash.

After 41 members are hospitalized in a riot, the Los Angeles-based International Brotherhood of Street Racers claims 10,000 members. The organization also claims to be race and gender integrated, patriotic, and drugfree.

Twenty percent of professional drag racers fail their first eye exams.

Architect Robert Venturi in an early postmodernist tract, *Complexity and Contradiction in Architecture*, attacks *God's Own Junkyard* and praises roadside architecture, especially the duck restaurant.

U.S. auto insurance losses pass $10 billion dollars.

Madison, Wisconsin, opens the first bus-only highway lane in the United States.

New York City closes Central Park roads to auto traffic on weekends.

Beach Boys sing of the 409-hp Chevy V-8: "She's real fine, my 409." Chevrolet also advertises that the muscle car is "cheaper than psychiatry."

Half a million Mustangs sold, mostly to baby boomers purchasing their first cars. They generate a billion dollar profit for Ford.

Sears-Roebuck and discount store chains are now selling speed equipment as part of a $500 million market.

Ford closes down experimental, company-owned high tech diagnostic centers that reported a high rate of consumer satisfaction because Ford dealers complain about the competition.

Most cars sold in the United States feature hard tops with no roll bar.

Oldsmobile is the first U.S. firm to offer front wheel drive.

At the insistence of the new federal safety regulators, Detroit car companies begin to offer bias-belted tires, standard in Europe, but only as an option.

New York's mayor seeks a ban on coal as a fuel after a Thanksgiving weekend killer smog.

Volkswagen fully automates body welding.

Ford wins the LeMans race after an expensive campaign to enhance its credibility in Europe.

First British custom car show.

Nissan opens a factory in Mexico.

When a racing motor designed by a college-trained engineer fails, Soichiro Honda tells him: "I hate college graduates." He forces the engineer to apologize to all the old factory mechanics whom the engineer had refused to consult.

Oil passes coal as the primary fuel in Western Europe, a sign of increasing automobility.

1967

Los Angeles has covered 35 percent of its ground area with roads, 24 percent with parking lots.

Los Angeles police pick up novelists Ray Bradbury and Aldous Huxley separately for a suspicious activity—walking in a suburban neighborhood.

Survey by *Motor Trend* suggests that 40 percent of U.S. marriage proposals take place in cars.

In *The Graduate* Dustin Hoffman drives an Alfa-Romeo Duetto Spider.

Roger Moore drives a Volvo sports car in TV's "The Saint."

Actress Jayne Mansfield dies in a car crash.

Santa Monica Freeway, Los Angeles, is the most heavily traveled highway in the world: 210,000 vehicles per day.

Making major streets one way and rigid parking law enforcement increase Manhattan traffic speeds over 20 percent and reduce pedestrian accidents.

Bradford Snell tells Congress that G.M. has collected $33 million in reparations and tax benefits from the U.S. government for bombing damage to its German plants during World War II.

Cadillac offers disc brakes, standard in the rest of the world, to customers, but only as an option.

G.M. builds its 100 millionth car; Ford its 70 millionth.

Ford integrates its European operations (12 years before G.M.). The integrated firm will de-emphasize production in Britain.

London's Pimlico neighborhood restricts auto entry.

British government forms and subsidizes British Leyland, a merger of B.M.C. and Leyland.

Honda's new microcar leads the domestic Japanese market.

Honda wins the Italian Grand Prix.

Mazda introduces the Wankel rotary-engined Model 110S.

Sweden switches to driving on the right. Iceland follows. In both countries large numbers of head-on collisions occur for several weeks following the change.

Hyundai Industries, South Korea, begins to produce cars with British Ford technology.

North Slope, Alaska, oil strike, largest oil find in U.S. history.

Japan begins to buy Soviet oil.

Grounded supertanker *Torrey Canyon* spills 119,000 tons of oil into the English Channel.

1968

Western European car production surpasses U.S. production.

American car registrations exceed the 100 million mark.

U.S. government forces manufacturers to put seat belts in cars.

In *Larson v. General Motors*, U.S. Court of Appeals rules out an 1842 English precedent and allows a driver injured by a poorly designed steering column to collect from G.M.

Largely to meet California air quality standards, American car makers adopt exhaust control systems.

Bullit, first film with multiple car-mounted cameras in a racing sequence. *Chitty, Chitty, Bang, Bang* is the first feature film to anthropomorphize cars. Jean-Luc Godard's *Weekend* contains the ultimate traffic jam sequence.

As Lyndon Johnson's popularity crashes, Lincoln presents him with a $500,000 Continental protected by two tons of armor plate.

U.S. mobile home production: 317,000 units.

Survey of American metro areas shows New York has the lowest proportion of auto commuters—67 percent. Peoria has the highest—98.7 percent.

Minneapolis converts Nicollet Street into a traffic-free mall.

McDonald's shifts from a slanted, suspended roof to a mansard roof on its restaurants.

Traffic deaths per 100,000 population: Lagos—27.5; Los Angeles—17.5; Paris—12.5; New York—10.7; London—10.2; Hamburg—8.1; Hong Kong—5.7.

Smith and Wesson begins to sell Breathalyzers to police departments.

Congress creates the Urban Mass Transit Authority.

New York City seeks to ban gypsy (unlicensed) cabs and independent bus lines in underserved black neighborhoods.

Gov. Nelson Rockefeller ends Robert Moses's career as New York's premier highway bureaucrat. In his 44-year career, Moses evicted over 250,000 people to build 1,003 kilometers of urban highways and other public works costing over $27 billion.

Ford offers radial tires as an option on some models, the first U.S. company to offer the 15-year-old technology.

Anti-trust action forces G.M. to sell the Euclid Road Machinery Company, acquired in 1953.

Trans-U.S. electric car race: winner takes 210 hours.

Breakthrough year for Japanese exports to the United States—182,000 units sold.

Japan has the highest auto fatality rate in the industrialized world, the United States the lowest.

After its driver dies in a crash at the French Grand Prix, Honda withdraws from racing.

French auto workers join a student-led revolt.

Paris Municipal Council rejects Peugeot's application to restore its neon sign, taken down in 1934, on the Eiffel Tower.

Academica di Belli Arti graduate Giorgetto Giugiaro starts Ital Design—the most important car styling firm of the late twentieth century.

1969

Congress requires environmental impact statements for new federal highways.

Central city protests end urban freeway construction in Philadelphia and Baltimore.

San Francisco exceeds federally allowable ozone standards for 67 days, six times the 1985 levels.

End of the hardtop: Chrysler puts roll bars in cars.

Lunar Exploratory Module, first car on the moon.

Average highway speed in the United States exceeds 60 mph (96 kph), an all-time high.

U.S. Air Force suffers more casualties from auto accidents than Vietnam War combat.

Limited access highway total: United States—62,400 kilometers; Germany—4,000; Sweden—1,920; France—1,760; Japan—1,632; Italy—1,600; United Kingdom—640.

Partying U.S. Senator Ted Kennedy leaves his campaign aide, Mary Jo Kopechne, to drown after driving his 1967 Oldsmobile Rocket 88 off a bridge, ending his presidential prospects.

Most American car buyers choose air conditioning as an option.

G.M. offers 175 body styles and 918 trim combinations.

Pontiac Firebird has a nonfunctional rear air foil, imitating race cars.

Steering column locks become standard on American cars.

Detroit produces its last rear-hinged door, an unsafe design.

"Smog-conspiracy" suit filed and settled in California.

Peak year for mobile homes in the United States with 412,000 units sold. This represents 34 percent of new single family homes.

Norman Mailer participates in a quasi-religious rite, burying a Ford to celebrate the end of one of his marriages and the end of a summer in Provincetown. While running for mayor of New York City, he proposes closing Wall Street for the stickball world series.

Easy Rider, the quintessential motorcycle movie.

"Then Came Bronson," TV show with a motorcycle-riding hero.

Anthropomorphic VW Beetle, Herbie, debuts in *The Love Bug*.

One-third of UAW members are black, only 7 percent of its leadership. Minority riots and alienation from unions now characterize both the European and U.S. industries.

Road Test Magazine honors an import for the first time, naming Nissan's Datsun 240-Z as car of the year.

Japan's government recalls 29 percent of Toyota's cars for defects.

Korea bans car imports to protect its nascent auto industry.

Fiat surpasses Volkswagen as the top European car maker.

Italian government makes a deal with Nissan to save Alfa-Romeo.

Italy prohibits a Ford takeover of Lancia. Fiat acquires Ferrari and Lancia.

When British Lord Burghley has his steel hip joint replaced, he places it on his Rolls-Royce as a hood ornament.

Soviets export 40 million tons of oil to Western Europe.

Santa Barbara offshore oil well spill covers 800 square miles (2,072 square kilometers).

In real dollars, U.S. energy costs are at the lowest point since the outbreak of World War II.

After 40 years of dry holes, oil found under the North Sea.

1970

Senator Gaylord Nelson proposes to ban the i.c. engine by 1975 because of pollution.

Clean Air Act passes Congress, requiring a 90 percent reduction in emissions by 1976, a goal largely attained.

Methanol-powered car wins a trans-U.S. clean air race (i.e., produces fewer emissions in a cross-country run than its competitors).

For the first time, more Americans live in suburbs (37.6%) than central cities (31.4%).

Percent of central city travel by car: Salt Lake City—95 percent; Los Angeles—62 percent; Detroit—53 percent; Boston—41 percent; Chicago—16 percent; Tokyo—16 percent; London—11 percent; Paris—11 percent; New York—6 percent.

New York highway builder Robert Moses: "A city without traffic is a ghost town."

For the first time, it is possible to drive from New York to San Francisco without encountering a traffic light.

Britain spends 34 percent of road-generated taxes on highways, compared to 100 percent for United States.

In Los Angeles, drunks cause 5,774 accidents, up from 3,500 in 1960 and 921 in 1940.

U.S. Department of Transportation (DOT) orders car makers to put front seat shoulder harnesses in 1974 cars.

After a secret meeting with Lee Iacocca, President Nixon rescinds the DOT order.

Average U.S. car is 5.6 years old, the youngest ever.

V-8s account for 85 percent of cars sold in the United States.

Cadillac offers an 8200-cc. engine, largest full scale production engine ever sold.

Auto companies begin to show black actors in ads for *Ebony*.

Plane crash kills Walter Reuther.

A.M.C. purchases Kaiser Jeep.

Ten percent Nixon surtax on Japanese imports to the United States.

Annual turnover rates for assembly line workers: Ford—25 percent; Volvo—35 percent; Fiat (foundry only)—100 percent.

Sixty-seven day strike against G.M. marks end of nearly 25 years of labor-management collaboration.

Australian state of Victoria requires drivers to wear seat belts.

Miriam Hargrove passes the U.K. driver's test on her 40th try.

For the first time, Japan, where less than 10 percent of the roads are paved, has more cars registered than trucks.

Smog crisis hospitalizes 8,000 in Tokyo, triggering Japan's first air pollution laws.

Peak year for U.S. oil production.

Libya successfully negotiates a better oil deal than other countries.

1971

Only 8 percent of New York City commuters travel in cars: Los Angeles—69 percent; Houston—86 percent; Milwaukee—95 percent.

New York mayor John Lindsay shuts down Madison Avenue for a pedestrian mall in a two-week experiment. Protests from cabbies prevent a permanent closing of the street.

Governor of Illinois claims that urban travel speeds are slower than in the previous century.

Wall Street Journal writes: "People today look at their cars as appliances to get them economically from place to place."

Mustang (eight inches longer, 600 pounds heavier than 1965) sales plummet. In Iacocca's words, it has become "a fat pig."

Henry Ford II: "Mini-cars mean mini-profits."

California psychologist convinces 15 people with clean driving records to affix Black Panther decals to their cars. Within three weeks police issue 33 citations to these drivers.

Federal Highway Administration authorizes European-style symbolic signs.

Several states ban studded tires, which cause excessive road wear.

Vanishing Point, the first cross-country car chase movie.

Steven Spielberg's first feature film, *Duel*, is the first car-portrayed-as-devil movie. Probably based on Stephen King's 1960s short story, *Christine*.

"Columbo" debuts—TV detective with a used car, a 1950s Studebaker.

For Rabbit Angstrom, the hero of John Updike's *Rabbit Redux,* who feels himself trapped in an unsatisfying marriage, his Ford's "stale air is his only heaven."

International Brotherhood of Street Racers organizes an 11,000-car park-in on Los Angeles' Van Nuys Boulevard during the Christmas season to protest the closing of the area's last drag strip.

Richard Petty becomes the first race driver to earn more than a million dollars in a season.

St. Paul, Minnesota, gives up on pedestrian safety, builds second story walkways in the central shopping area.

G.M. successfully tests, then abandons, a drunk-resistant starting device.

In *Bell v. Burson*, the U.S. Supreme Court rules that driving is a property right and licenses cannot be revoked without a hearing.

Under pressure from G.M., American tire firms, which had resisted making the radial tire because of its long life, begin to produce them in large quantities.

G.M. buys 34 percent of financially troubled Isuzu.

Signs of Japan's emergence as a car-making power: Japan surpasses Germany in automobile production. Toyota sells its ten millionth export. Chrysler begins to buy into Mitsubishi.

European Common Market adopts clean air standards for cars.

Angry West Germans successfully protest a proposed 100 kph speed limit.

For the first time, most British households own a car.

Saab introduces headlight windshield wipers.

Opel sells more cars to Germans than Volkswagen.

Fiat builds a massive factory for the USSR. Its 1.25-mile-long assembly line is the longest ever built.

Fiat introduces the 127, first production front wheel drive car profitably made, 12 years after British Motors pioneered the concept.

Shah of Iran celebrates what he claims is the 2,500th anniversary of his dynasty by spending over $100 million on a party in Persopolis. Maxim's serves over 25,000 bottles of wine to the guests, including 50 heads of state.

Britain ends its defense commitments east of Suez, leaving the United States as guardian of the Gulf sheikdoms.

Texas Railroad Commission ends its quota system, marking the end of surplus American oil production capacity.

1972

All-time high: 56,528 Americans die in auto accidents.

DOT, at the auto industry's request, mandates interlocking seat belts for 1974 models.

Careful engineering/medical analysis of New Zealand automobile accidents show that seat belt wearers have 40 percent fewer crashes than non-wearers.

President Nixon gives Soviet premier Brezhnev a Cadillac.

Rush hour traffic speeds (kph): Salt Lake City—43; Singapore—34; London—33; Paris—27; Manila—18; Lagos—17.

Paris Peripherique (beltway) completed. Paris adopts parking meters to cope with 120,000 illegally parked cars.

Bay Area Rapid Transit, the first U.S. subway since World War II, opens.

"M*A*S*H" character Radar O'Reilly tries to mail home a jeep one part at a time.

Boston massage parlors begin to advertise "house calls" and limousine services.

Boston abandons its Inner Loop highway plan.

Big Daddy Garlits unionizes professional drag racers.

Hot Rod Magazine makes its only mention of the Vietnam War, carrying Garlits's attack on the Pentagon.

New York's Museum of Modern Art adds a Ferdinand Porsche-designed 1947 Cisitala 202GT to its permanent collection.

Recreational vehicle sales in the United States crack the half million mark.

In the middle of a fitness craze, Americans buy more bicycles than cars.

Postmodern architect James Wine argues in *Architectural Forum* that "form follows fantasy, not function," praising roadside architecture, especially the duck-shaped restaurant.

Economists associated with Ralph Nader suggest that the American market should be adequate for 12 to 33 manufacturers, but that the Detroit oligopoly's control over dealers restricts new manufacturing firms.

Peak year for British car production.

G.M. engineers report that the new front wheel drive Volkswagen Golf (Rabbit in the United States) is the wave of the future, but G.M. management rejects similar designs.

German author R. Dahl's *Beginning of the End of the Car* attacks "the death wish" of German drivers.

Average age of junked German cars has dropped from 13 to 10 years, despite lower fuel economy per year, per car. Comparable figure: United States—6; Denmark—14; Switzerland—8.

Ford signs an agreement with Phillips (Holland) to develop Stirling cycle engines.

Renault markets polypropylene car bumpers.

Humaine, Trop Humaine, the powerful French documentary, depicts a Citroën assembly line.

Saab switches from assembly lines to production teams in factories. Volvo follows.

Fiat introduces numerically controlled factory robots.

Not one entry finishes the first Ivory Coast rally.

Murati factory (India's attempt to build a "people's car") opens. It will fail within five years.

About this date *bo-su-zuko*, Japanese adolescent hot rod gangs, appear.

Lagos, Nigeria, site of the world's highest pedestrian fatality rate, has 1.5 million people, 50,000 cars, and no working traffic lights.

Standard of New Jersey changes its brand name from Esso to Exxon at a cost of $100 million.

Supertanker *Sea Star* grounds, spilling 115,000 tons of oil into the Gulf of Oman.

Arab oil ministers at an OPEC meeting include graduates of Harvard, NYU, Cornell, Washington and Wisconsin.

1973

Arab oil producers impose a ban on exports of oil to the U.S., because of United States aid to Israel in the Yom Kippur War.

President Nixon signs legislation reducing the speed limit from 70 mph (112 kph) to 55 mph (88 kph).

U.S. National Guard called out to open highways blocked by convoys of truckers seeking higher speed limits.

U.S.-made cars average 5.8 kpl, about half 1949 levels; imports—9.4 kpl.

Ten thousand service stations in the United States close because of the gas crisis.

Congress taps the Interstate Highway Fund for some mass transit.

Two millionth American auto fatality.

Sixty-five vehicles collide in a chain reaction accident on the foggy New Jersey Turnpike, killing nine.

Seat belt interlock mandatory in the United States.

U.S. government bans lead in gasoline.

Detroit car makers produce 9.7 million cars, their all-time peak.

Hot Rod Magazine proposes a Hot Rodders Bill of Rights, attacks Nader, seat belt rules and anti-pollution laws, and tries to form a lobbying group modeled on the Sierra Club.

Shirley Muldowney's dragster catches fire, welding her eyelids together. She will return to racing after plastic surgery.

Average journey to work for Manhattan lawyers exceeds 32 kilometers.

Boston opens Quincy Market, a downtown restoration imitative of suburban malls. Within three years, it will draw more visitors annually than Disney World and trigger a wave of downtown restoration mall building.

Dump truck falls through the elevated West Side Highway in New York City, permanently closing down the busy road.

Cambridge, Massachusetts, becomes the first U.S. city to limit parking to residents.

George Lucas' film, *American Graffiti*, romanticizes the 1950s cruising style. European adolescents will imitate the movie.

Performance artist Craig Stecyk sets a 1959 Cadillac on fire on the streets of Bel Air, an elite Los Angeles suburb, entitles the flaming "sculpture" *Ignition Problems*.

Executive John DeLorean resigns from G.M., announcing: "The automobile industry has lost its masculinity."

Over 100 million cars registered in Western Europe, over 10 million in South America.

London traffic jam forces Prime Minister Edward Heath to abandon his limousine and walk to work.

British police adopt radar to trap speeders.

Tariff barriers for cars have fallen below 10 percent in most industrial nations.

Volkswagen Beetle production ends at Wolfsburg, West Germany, after 25 years and 16.2 million cars. It has surpassed the Model T as the best-selling model ever, but is too polluting and unsafe for current standards.

West Germany provides cash to almost bankrupt Volkswagen.

Soichiro Honda retires, complaining that he has gotten too old to drink all night with his workers.

Brazil promotes ethanol (a sugar cane byproduct) for fuel.

1974

Congress repeals the seat-belt interlock law after massive public protests.

Probably the worst year for quality in the European and U.S. car industries. Ford, Chevrolet, Chrysler, A.M.C., Fiat, Volkswagen, Triumph and even Volvo face major recalls for rust, engines leaking gas fumes and bad brakes.

G.M. sells air bags as options, but stops in 1976 because few consumers buy them.

American car firms finally switch completely to radial tires.

Because of the 88-kph speed limit, U.S traffic fatalities decline from 4.28 to 3.44 per 100 million miles (1.6 million kilometers) traveled.

Ant Farm, an art collaborative, builds *Cadillac Ranch* (ten Cadillacs with front ends buried and rear ends elevated) at Amarillo, Texas.

In E. L. Doctorow's novel, *Ragtime*, Coalhouse Walker's Ford symbolizes wealth for African Americans. Suburban firefighters trash it to show the black Walker his place.

Robert Pirsig publishes *Zen and the Art of Motorcycle Maintenance*, an Odyssey theme book about father-son bonding on a motorcycle trip.

Harry and Tonto: the first geriatric car chase movie.

Arthur Fonzarelli seeks to make motorcyclists socially acceptable on the TV series "Happy Days."

"Rockford Files," signature car a gold Camaro.

Truck Stop Women, the first soft core pornographic trucking movie.

Westway, the proposed successor to the collapsed West Side Highway, carries an estimated price of $15,000 per inch or $1.52 billion per kilometer.

Bus lane in the Lincoln Tunnel, New York City, carries 25,800 people per rush hour.

Roman authorities buttress the Colosseum with scaffolding, fearing a collapse caused by traffic vibration.

California scientists discover depletion of the earth's ozone layer. Fluoro-carbons from car air conditioners create much of the problem.

Honda presents G.M. with a Vega refitted with a Honda cylinder head. The car has better gas economy and can meet EPA standards without catalytic converters. When G.M. ignores the gift, Honda decides to enter the U.S. market.

G.M. employs 1,700 designers. Honda employs 3.

In a recession, Toyota sends its workers out to sell its inventory door-to-door, rather than lay them off.

British Labour party cancels motorway construction in the London area, but rejects congestion pricing.

Volkswagen acquires a plant in the United States to produce the new Rabbit.

Germany deals with auto industry layoffs by deporting "guest workers."

Volvo buys the Dutch firm, DAF.

Japanese banks bail out Toyo-Kogo (Mazda) after its investment in the gas-guzzling Wankel rotary engine proves a major mistake.

Hyundai (Korea) shows its first export car at the Turin Motor Show.

Trans-Amazonian coast-to-coast highway (5,375 kilometers) completed.

Price of crude oil is four times 1972 levels. The recession blamed on oil price shock leads to a 5 percent decline in U.S. incomes.

President Nixon establishes a three-tier control system for oil prices.

Henry Kissinger on energy economics: "Don't talk about barrels of oil. They might as well be bottles of Coca Cola. I don't understand."

First quarter profits up 52 percent (Shell) to 123 percent (Texaco) for the major oil companies. On "Sixty Minutes," the shah of Iran accuses the oil companies of creating an artificial gas shortage.

Soviet Union becomes the world's largest producer and refiner of crude oil.

1975

One million cars stolen in the United States, a record.

Bruce Springsteen, who owns a 1957 Chevy convertible painted with orange flames, releases his first hit, "Born to Run," which emphasizes a working class car-as-escape theme.

Five years after his first, Dave Thomas opens his thousandth Wendy's franchise restaurant.

Congress mandates fuel economy standards for cars (CAFE).

DOT puts off the passive restraint requirement to 1976.

Congress tells DOT that it cannot withhold road funds from states refusing to pass mandatory helmet laws. Repeal of the helmet law follows in many states.

Chrysler products contain solid state components and electronic spark control. This premature innovation is plagued by failures as Chrysler quality, already poor, further declines.

Joe Garagiola launches first factory-to-customer price rebate program as Chrysler wrestles with a huge, unwanted inventory.

All American car manufacturers adopt catalytic converters.

"Baseball, apple pie, hot dogs, and Chevrolet."

Half the garbage trucks in the United States have compactors.

"Convoy," a trucking song, tops the hit parade in both Britain and the United States.

Meat Loaf's "Paradise by the Dashboard Light" tops the record charts, making Phil Rizzuto a major rock star.

Nashville evangelist Jimmy Snow begins a citizens band radio ministry for truckers.

Sculptor Alexander Calder customizes a BMW, adding, among other things, tail fins.

Limited access highway distance: West Germany—6,000 kilometers; Italy—5,000; France—3,000; United Kingdom—1,380.

Datsun (Nissan) and Toyota surpass Volkswagen in U.S. sales.

U.S. tire firms start to abandon their European factories.

Taxes as a percentage of fuel prices: United States—18 percent; Japan—28 percent; Europe—45 percent.

Renault buys Citroën.

West German central bank purchases 29 percent of Daimler-Benz to keep it out of the hands of the shah of Iran. The Bundestag bans such foreign takeovers.

Britain puts a cap on Japanese imports. France follows in 1977 and the United States in 1981.

Jaguar's new 12-cylinder engines frequently stall while the car is in motion.

Britain nationalizes bankrupt British Leyland.

Fiat hires women assembly line workers for the first time.

Honda's CVCC (stratified charge) engine is the first to comply with new U.S. Clean Air Act requirements.

Hyundai factory opens in South Korea, producing the Giugiaro-styled, Mitsubishi-engined Pony.

1976

Causes of fatal accidents in the United States: 33 percent speeding, 23 percent failure to yield right of way, 22 percent swerved off the road. About 50 percent are alcohol related, and pedestrians account for only 18 percent of the fatalities.

All Detroit cars require unleaded gasoline. In the next six years, concentrations of lead in United States urban atmospheres decline 60 percent.

Recently created car pool and bus lanes on Los Angeles freeways abandoned after public uproar.

Washington, D.C., subway system opened.

DOT abandons passive restraint requirements.

Persons per car ratio in the United States dips below two.

Houston Astrodome has 50,000 seats, 30,000 parking spots.

Honda Accord introduced into the United States—first Japanese car to appeal in styling and power to the middle and upper segments of the United States market.

Michelin opens a factory in South Carolina.

Peak of the citizens band radio fad in the United States: six million sold.

Big Three stop making convertibles, because consumers prefer air conditioning.

Janet Guthrie becomes the first woman to qualify for the Indianapolis 800.

National Security Agency starts monitoring car telephone conversations in Moscow from a space satellite.

Ford of Europe introduces the German-designed Fiesta Eurocar with an English engine block, French transmission, Irish carburetor, and Spanish engine machinery.

Germany mandates wearing seat belts.

Australian state of Victoria introduces random breath tests and a mandatory seat belt law. Auto accident fatalities decline by 38 percent.

1977

Jimmy Carter *walks* in his inaugural parade.

Carter administration overrules DOT. Passive restraints mandatory by 1982.

U.S. Environmental Pollution Agency forces states to set up exhaust inspection programs and prods cities to ban some parking.

President Carter limits off-road vehicles in national parks.

Top year for recalls, nearly 11 million U.S.-manufactured vehicles recalled.

Oldsmobile owners complain because G.M. is putting Chevrolet engines in new models.

Of new cars made in the United States, 95 percent have automatic transmissions, 80 percent have air conditioning, and 77 percent have V-8 engines.

Chrysler begins to market Mitsubishi Colts under the Chrysler name.

Former U-2 spy plane pilot, Francis Gary Powers, killed in a helicopter crash while covering traffic for a Los Angeles radio station.

Following her will, heirs bury Los Angeleno Sandra West in her Ferrari.

Peak year for car films. Hollywood makes 15, including *Heartbreak, King of the Road* and *Smoky and the Bandit*.

In the TV series "CHIPS" teenage heartthrob Eric Estrada plays a California motorcycle cop whose personal car is a gold Camaro.

Shirley Muldowney wins the national drag-racing championship, breaking 250 mph (400 kph) for a quarter mile.

A. J. Foyt, first to win Indy 800 four times.

Merle Haggard sings the top country and western hit: "The Rambling Man."

Winston-Salem shell-shaped station (see 1929) placed on the National Register of Historic Places.

Chevrolet fails to market the Nova successfully in Latin America, in part because Nova means "no go" in Spanish.

Chain reaction accident with 140 vehicles in Sao Paulo, Brazil, kills 14.

Belgian drivers have the worst safety record in Western Europe.

German cities have 377 car-free streets.

Tokyo begins installation of a $28 million computerized traffic control system that it believes will increase traffic speeds 10 percent.

British Leyland has over 700 strikes, the result of negotiating with 22 different craft unions in a time of decline.

French textile workers at the Schlumpf brothers' factories in Mulhouse take over the brothers' fabulous auto collection when the brothers shut down their factories and flee to Switzerland with embezzled profits. The workers open the collection as a museum.

Alaska pipeline finished.

1978

Over 380 million motor cars registered in the world (146 million in the United States).

Passenger kilometers per liter in the United States (urban): auto—9.4; bus—71.7; railroad—35.8.

During the previous 10 years, over 71 million United States cars recalled for repairs.

National Highway and Transportation Safety Administration (NHTSA) forces Firestone to replace *eight million* "500" belted tires.

After considerable infighting, lawyers replace engineers in most of the top spots at NHTSA. They prefer recalls (politically popular with constituents) to setting design standards, a legally troublesome process. The latter offers a better route to safety because mechanical defects only account for 13 percent of traffic fatalities.

Nader's Raiders publicize the gas tanks in Ford Pintos, which explode in rear-end collisions.

Blue Lake, Minnesota—the supposed last kilometer of the Interstate System completed.

Mercedes owner Robert O'Reilly of Olympia, Washington claims his 1957 Mercedes has traveled 1.9 million kilometers.

Fannie Turner (77 years old) passes the written test for her driver's license after 104 attempts.

"Dukes of Hazzard" TV show begins 1960s muscle car nostalgia with its signature car, a souped-up 1960s Dodge Charger called "The General Lee."

Chrysler falls to 13th in world auto sales, behind Lada (USSR).

Plymouth Horizon/Dodge Omni brings front wheel drive to the American economy car market, with a French Simca design.

Peugeot-Citroën purchases Chrysler's European operations.

Ford introduces electronic engine controls.

Henry Ford II fires Lee Iacocca.

Improved digital computers allow Mercedes's engineer Heinz Leiber to introduce reliable antilock brakes, modeled on those adopted by airplanes in the 1960s.

Japanese car sales lag in the United States as oil prices decline and devaluation of the United States dollar makes United States labor cheaper.

UAW membership peaks at 760,000.

First plastic monocoque car: Lotus Elite.

Amoco Cadiz tanker sinks, spilling 253,000 tons of oil and fouling 160 kilometers of Brittany coastline.

1979

World oil consumption peaks at 65 million barrels per day.

Second gas crisis forces drivers into gas lines. The first gasoline riot ensues in Levittown, Pennsylvania.

Livermore Lab, California, tests solar cars.

Car buff Mike Shetley makes the much ballyhooed claim that his Shetley-mobile can average 110 mpg (46.9 kpl). EPA tests show only 14.4 kpl with pollution much greater than allowable limits.

Eleven million U.S. motor vehicles junked—a record.

UAW offers Chrysler concessions, breaking a 40-year tradition of identical contracts for the Big Three firms.

Ten million Americans live in mobile homes.

Japanese control one-fifth of the U.S. auto market. They freeze exports, fearing a U.S. tariff.

"Dallas," the popular television show, portrays J. R. Ewing as the archetypal oil millionaire.

Gary Numan sings "Cars," a paranoid pop song about the security of being in his car.

Since 1962 proportion of German cars with engines over 1500 cc. has risen from 13 percent to 51 percent. Average daily car travel has increased from 13.6 kilometers to 22 kilometers. Germans do 80 percent of their vacation and leisure travel in cars. Over 58 percent of women and 17 percent of men have no driver's license.

American Motors and Renault (46% owner of A.M.C.) agree to produce the Renault-designed Alliance in the United States.

British Leyland obtains the right to produce Hondas for the European market.

Ford buys 25 percent of financially troubled Toyo-Kogo (Mazda).

Ford overseas sales are 38 percent of its total, G.M.—19 percent.

Ten firms control 91 percent of European Common Market auto production.

Humber Bridge, England: 1,410 meters.

Volga Motor Works turns out 600,000 Fiat-designed cars for the Soviet market.

Hong Kong driver pays HK$336,000 for a license plate with the lucky number 6.

Two oil tankers collide off Trinidad, spill 300,000 tons. An offshore Mexican oil well at Ixtoc spills 600,000 tons.

1980

Japanese car production surpasses U.S. production. Worldwide, the auto accounts for 2,220 kilometers of travel per person, 6 million jobs, and 250,000 fatal accidents.

Ms. C. Lightner starts Mothers Against Drunk Driving (MADD) in Fair Oaks, California, after her thirteen-year-old daughter Cari is killed by a drunk driver while walking to church.

Most U.S. households own more than one car.

U.S. census shows that the average journey to work has declined since 1970, reflecting the increasing move of jobs to the suburbs, where two-thirds of Americans work.

Toyota introduces the motorized, automatic seat belt.

Chrysler, facing bankruptcy, gets a government bail out loan.

Chrysler ends overseas operation, selling its Australian and Asian subsidiaries to Mitsubishi.

Airplane competition cuts into intercity bus travel in the U.S.

L.A. has 231 days with unhealthy air quality, 98 more than New York City, 223 more than Tampa.

Urban bus routes cover 195,200 kilometers, twice the 1960 level.

Massachusetts has the highest auto theft rate in the United States, South Dakota the lowest.

In the "Magnum, P.I." TV series, Tom Selleck drives a Ferrari.

Springsteen's new album, "The River," moves away from car and woman themes, although it contains a few songs like "Cadillac Ranch."

Delores Drive-in, Beverly Hills, is declared a historic landmark.

Society for Commercial Architecture runs tour of historic all-night roadside diners.

Nevada casino magnate William Harrah dies. His heirs begin to auction off his 1,200-vehicle antique car collection. The prize of the collection, a Bugatti Royale, will sell to Domino's Pizza owner Tom Monaghan for $8 million in 1986.

Ford introduces the German-designed, Japanese-engined Escort, designed for the world market.

G.M. recalls its new generation of front wheel drive cars to repair defects.

G.M., historically the industry leader in air bag technology, becomes their leading opponent and will be the most sluggish of United States firms in installing them.

G.M. loses $763 million, its first annual loss in 60 years.

G.M. announces soon-aborted plans to build 100,000 electric cars a year.

Former G.M. executive John DeLorean arrested for allegedly seeking a $60 million cocaine deal to finance his car company. The courts later acquit him because of police entrapment.

Volkswagen exports to the United States dip under 100,000 units.

British manufacturers are not competitive now that Britain has joined the Common Market, and it imports more cars than it produces.

Low wage Spain produces over a million cars, almost all for foreign companies. Ford of Britain and Vauxhall (G.M.'s British subsidiary) have moved almost all manufacturing operations to Spain. They only assemble and sell cars in Britain.

British Leyland and Fiat win strikes, ending shop floor control by union shop stewards. Fiat lays off 23,000 workers after the strike.

Enzo Ferrari dies.

Per kilometer of travel: Spain has the highest death rate in auto accidents in the industrialized world, Norway the lowest.

Datsun 240-Z is the top-selling sports car in the world. Over 720,000 sold to date.

Mazda reintroduces the RX-7 with a Wankel rotary engine. After making one million rotaries, Mazda has finally solved the rotor seal problem.

St. Gotthard Tunnel, Switzerland—16.4 kilometers, world's longest vehicular tunnel.

Exxon loses a billion dollars on oil shale development.

Iraq-Iran War breaks the OPEC cartel. Both sides will sell petroleum at a reduced price to pay for the war.

The A. M. Browns, with their children, Hope, Archie and Jim, live in Westchester County, N. Y. Like many other suburbanites they say:

"I cover 500 miles a week between my home and my office," says Mr. Brown. "I travel over all kinds of roads, so comfort is important to me; another thing is economy—you really get both in a Ford."...Ford's new spring and shock absorber action reduces front-end road shock up to 80% and the Power Pilot gives high-compression performance on "regular."

"Two Fords are a must with us!"

"When the children were small," says Mr. Brown, "one Ford handled our driving needs perfectly. But now two Fords are a must with us. We chose Fords because we felt they offered by far the best value besides being the most comfortable and easiest to handle."...When they sell their Fords, the Browns should find they're worth more, too. Used car prices show Fords hold on to their value longer than any other cars.

"We live miles from a shopping center which means a lot of hauling and a station wagon was essential for us."...The Ford Country Sedan hauls a half ton with ease yet it converts into an 8-passenger sedan in seconds.

"My wife can park without half trying, our Ford's so easy to handle."...Now with Ford's new Master-Guide power steering available on V-8's, parking, and all driving, is easier still. Master-Guide provides the muscles—you merely guide the car.

"No more 'Who gets the car?' sessions in our house! Our Country Sedan is always there for the family use."...The Country Sedan is powered by the only V-8 in the low-price field. Of course, if you prefer sixes, Ford's Six is the most modern six

you can buy. If your family needs two cars, why not talk it over with your Ford Dealer? Remember, you can buy two fine cars for the price of one if they're Fords, and the chances are the car you own today may well provide the down payment.

Worth more when you buy it...
worth more when you sell it!

Ford

Ford marketed station wagons as second cars to 1950 suburbanites. Note the gender division of cars and the availability of big V-8 engines. From the J. Walter Thompson Collection, Duke University, courtesy of Ford Motor Company.

The 1955 Ford Skyliner with an early example of the sunroof offered power
windows, power brakes, power steering, power seats and an automatic shift. All
were symbols of luxury and youth. All increased fuel consumption. From
the J. Walter Thompson Collection, Duke University, courtesy of Ford Motor
Company.

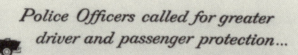

Police Officers called for greater driver and passenger protection...

FORD answered with
LIFEGUARD DESIGN

Police authorities have pointed out that accident injuries could be reduced by changes in automobile design.

More than two years ago Ford, in cooperation with police safety experts, universities and medical associations started a program of research and testing so a safer car could be built. The result? Lifeguard Design in the '56 Ford.

For example, the steering post was found to be a major hazard to the driver in accidents. So Ford designed a new steering wheel that actually takes up most of the shock of impact. Occupants hitting hard surfaces within the car—or being thrown out — are the other important factors in accidents. Ford helps protect passengers against these hazards with new double-grip door latches, double-swivel rear-view mirror, optional padding for control panel and sun visors and optional floor-anchored seat belts.

FORD Division of FORD MOTOR COMPANY

Seat belts help keep driver and passengers from being thrown from their seats, in the event of an accident.

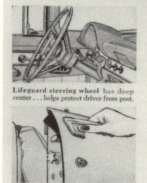

Lifeguard steering wheel has deep center . . . helps protect driver from post.

Lifeguard door locks give extra protection from doors opening under impact.

Lifeguard cushioning for instrument panel and sun visors helps lessen injuries from impact against hard surfaces, in case of an accident.

In 1956 Ford became the first firm to offer a safety package as an option. Traffic fatalities were soaring, in part because horsepower was outpacing braking. Ford abandoned the package because it seemed to scare customers away from its products. From the J. Walter Thompson Collection, Duke University, courtesy of Ford Motor Company

Liveliest engines in town . . .

Yessir, when it comes to V-8's, there's just no catching up with Ford. Ford has built more than any-body else . . . *by millions*. Take the 9-passenger Country Squire above. Here's cat-scalding V-8 dash. Thunderbird V-8 dash. Whisks a full load smartly along with a powerful margin of safety. And does it on *regular* gas, for regular savings. Four new "hurry up" Ford engines now await your orders. Take your pick . . . and feel a real blaze start in your heart. (P.S. The Fire Engine, too, is a Ford V-8.)

NEW FORD GALAXIE CLUB VICTORIA—THUNDERBIRD STYLING IN A 5-PASSENGER, 2-DOOR HARDTOP

Beautiful new award-winning proportions · Exclusive luxury lounge interiors with full living-room comfort for all six people · New Diamond Lustre finish never needs waxing · Safety Glass all around · Standard aluminized mufflers for twice the life · 4000 miles between oil changes

WORLD'S MOST BEAUTIFULLY PROPORTIONED CARS

During the horsepower race, even sedate cars like this 1959 Ford station wagon were marketed for their power and speed. From the J. Walter Thompson Collection, Duke University, courtesy of Ford Motor Company.

FORD PRESENTS—

the world's newest fine cars... LINCOLN *for* '59

The MARK IV Continental Limousine — Integral frame-and-body construction offers unexcelled passenger comfort. This Limousine becomes the standard against which luxury motoring will be judged.

EDSEL *for* '59

Edsel Corsair 4-door Sedan. In 1959 Edsel continues to be the most distinctive car in its class, offering more genuine styling, mechanical and performance luxuries than cars costing much more.

MERCURY *for* '59

Mercury Park Lane 2-door Hardtop. Longer and lovelier — with handsome swept-back windshield — and instantly responding, yet economical power, tailored to the performance you need.

You command the world's most dynamic cars in the new Lincoln, Edsel and Mercury!

Each of these cars has its own distinctive quality of excitement. There is the daring use of sculptured steel in the Lincoln — with a minimum of ornamentation. There is matchless individuality in the Edsel's grille, and in the sweeping planes of its decks. There is brisk, clean purposefulness in the incomparable elegance of the Mercury.

And the dynamic performance of these cars fulfills the exciting promise of their looks . . . eager, easy power at your fingertips, instant response to your steering commands, a beautifully balanced, road-hugging ride.

Wherever you live... you get more for your money in *any* Ford-built product

THE WORLD-WIDE

F**O**RD

COMPANIES

Ford-built products include cars, trucks, tractors, industrial engines, genuine replacement parts: Meteor • Monarch / Popular • Anglia • Prefect • Consul • Zephyr • Zodiac • Thames • Fordson Major and Dexta Tractors / Taunus • FK Truck / MARK IV Continental • Mercury • Edsel • Lincoln • Ford • Thunderbird • Ford Tractor and Implements

In 1959 Ford marketed the Lincoln, Edsel and Mercury to distinct social class niches. Ford's relatively subdued tail fins were the key to distinguishing between models. From the J. Walter Thompson Collection, Duke University, courtesy of Ford Motor Company.

Put away the boring bar—

we've done it for you!

Now we've scooped out Fairlane's V-8 to 289 cubes . . . 271 h.p.! This, friend, is a real stormer! Solid lifters, 4-barrel carb, the whole bit. Can you think of better news for the guy who wants solid, off-the-line punch from a gem-size power plant? Tie this savage little winder to a four-speed floor shift, tuck it into Fairlane's no-fat body shell, and you've got a going-handling combo that's mighty hard to beat...and we mean that both ways! The factory overbore is better than doing it yourself . . . you know the cores are in the right place, and the bottom end is tested to take the kind of rpm this V-8 churns out! So put away the boring bar and check your friendly Ford Dealer; he'll show you what 289 cubes can do.

America's liveliest, most care-free cars!

FORD
FALCON · FAIRLANE · FORD · THUNDERBIRD

FOR 60 YEARS THE SYMBOL OF DEPENDABLE PRODUCTS

Ford

MOTOR COMPANY

Ford advertised souped-up, 289-cubic-horsepower engines in *Hot Rod Magazine* in 1963, presumably for street-racing purposes. From the J. Walter Thompson Collection, Duke University, courtesy of Ford Motor Company.

WHAT'S HAPPENED TO FALCON

EVERYTHING!
AND YET...

Early this year we put a 164-hp V-8 in a new kind of Falcon called the Sprint, and entered the stiffest winter road test we could find . . . the 2,500-mile Monte Carlo Rallye. We didn't know what would happen . . . but happen it did.

First, no one dreamed all the Rallye cars would have to experience the worst winter in decades. Snow, below zero temperatures, and the most demanding terrain in Europe took their toll. Two thirds of the 296 cars that started, failed to reach Monaco.

A lot of experts told us that the Falcon V-8's, untried as they were, could not hope to finish the Rallye with the best of weather. But not only did two Falcon Sprints finish, they placed first and second in their class. But there were more surprises (for

everyone) in store. Against all competition, regardless of class, the lead Sprint went on to take first in the final six performance legs.

We honestly didn't know the Falcon Sprint would do this well. But it showed us a Falcon with our new 164-hp V-8 is a car that can perform with the best of them. So a lot has happened to Falcon, and yet . . .

A six-cylinder Falcon has just finished the Mobil Economy Run and finished first in its class. It had to take a lot of punishment, too . . . 2,500 miles from Los Angeles to Detroit over mountains, deserts, and long stretches of superhighways. But the nickel-nursing ways of the all-time Economy Champ took all comers in its class.

So you see something has happened to the Falcon. It can be what you want it to be . . . a V-8 that travels in the same circle as Europe's performance kings . . . or a Six that can travel cross-country on a budget. *There's* something to put into your compact.

**AMERICA'S LIVELIEST,
MOST CARE-FREE CARS**

FORD

FALCON · FAIRLANE · FORD · THUNDERBIRD

FOR 60 YEARS THE SYMBOL
OF DEPENDABLE PRODUCTS

Ford

MOTOR COMPANY

Ford offered the compact Falcon as a response to Volkswagen's American success during the 1957–58 recession. Ford steadily upsized the car. This 1963 Falcon was 14 inches longer than the original and offered an optional 164-hp engine. From the J. Walter Thompson Collection, Duke University, courtesy of Ford Motor Company.

Two weeks ago this man was a bashful schoolteacher in a small mid-western city. **Add Mustang.** Now he has three steady girls, is on first name terms with the best headwaiter in town, is society's darling. All the above came with his Mustang. So did bucket seats, full wheel covers, wall-to-wall carpeting, padded dash, vinyl upholstery, and more. Join the Mustangers! Enjoy a lot of *dolce vita* at a low, low price.

Best year yet to go Ford!
Test Drive Total Performance '65

FORD

MUSTANG·FALCON·FAIRLANE·FORD·THUNDERBIRD

The 1964 Mustang was the most popular 1960s model and its ad tried to capitalize on the baby boomers' sexual revolution. From the J. Walter Thompson Collection, Duke University, courtesy of Ford Motor Company.

Earns its living as a truck. Doubles as a second car.

You're ahead in a Ford.

Look it over. Every inch of this handsome '67 Ford has the bold, broad look of a solid truck. It's built for work, but you'd never suspect it behind the wheel. Seats are wider, deeper, more comfortable. Cabs are the roomiest of any pickup. Four inches more shoulder space and a swept-away dash give generous room for three husky men. A new longer wheelbase and Ford's exclusive Twin-I-Beam suspension deliver a ride only a car can match. What's more, Twin-I-Beam's forged steel construction gives you the most rugged independent suspension made. Put a tough '67 Ford pickup on your job—let it prove that a hard-working truck needn't be work to drive.

The 1967 Ford pickup was designed to double as a family car with amenities like automatic transmission. Especially in the South, pickups became a blue-collar masculine symbol, not just a utility vehicle. Note the admiring carhop (waitress at roadside restaurant who brought food to the vehicles). From the J. Walter Thompson Collection, Duke University, courtesy of Ford Motor Company.

As the quality of American cars declined, Detroit desperately turned to more explicit sexual marketing and race-car-type styling as this ad for a 1971 Mustang shows. From the J. Walter Thompson Collection, Duke University, courtesy of Ford Motor Company.

PINTO
Ford

What you need to know about import-size cars depends on what you expect from one.

If you're looking for precise handling and resistance to cross winds, you'll need to know that Ford's new little Pinto has a wider stance than any economy import and is the only car in its class with rack-and-pinion steering (like in Porsche and Jaguar).

If you're looking for performance for freeway driving, you'll need to know that Pinto's 1.6 litre engine has 75 horsepower compared to VW's 60. Or you can get Pinto's 2 litre engine with overhead cam and Webber carburetion that develops 100 horsepower—which is more than either Toyota Corona or Datsun.

If you want real economy, you'll need to know that Pinto averaged over 25 mpg in simulated city and suburban driving, that the steering is lubed for life, that it

needs oil changes only twice a year. And that its suspension needs lubrication only once in three years (or 36,000 miles).

If you're interested in durability, you'll be happy to know that Pinto has parts you'd expect to find in bigger, stronger cars. So it will run quieter, longer.

If you want heavy-duty brakes, you should know that you can get floating-caliper front disc brakes on Pinto.

If you want driving ease, you need to know that Pinto offers you SelectShift—the three-speed automatic transmission that lets you downshift or hold lower gears for better control.

If you're looking for room inside where inches really count, you'll need to

know that Pinto has more front leg room, more front and rear shoulder room, and more rear-seat knee room than VW, Toyota Corona, or Datsun 510 and Pinto's door is wider than any of the smaller imports for easy rear-seat entry-exit.

Pinto is import priced and sized, but gives you more...more room inside, greater driving ease, better handling, and the durability you want in a small car.

So if you expect more, then Pinto may be all you need to know about import-size cars.

A little better idea from Ford.

Detroit responded to the quality, energy and safety crises of the 1970s with a second generation of compact cars. Ford advertised this 1979 Pinto as an "import-sized" car. The new compacts proved unreliable and unsafe, however. From the J. Walter Thompson Collection, Duke University, courtesy of Ford Motor Company.

As the large car market collapsed, companies began marketing truck-based utility vehicles like this 1979 Bronco as family cars. These big vehicles proved immensely popular during the economic revival of the 1980s and 1990s. From the J. Walter Thompson Collection, Duke University, courtesy of Ford Motor Company.

On the third try, Detroit finally got compact cars right. The German-designed, Japanese-engined 1981 Escort was Detroit's first successful response to the Japanese invasion of U.S. auto markets. From the J. Walter Thompson Collection, Duke University, courtesy of Ford Motor Company.

7

Revival:
1981–1994

1981

President Reagan tells the Detroit Economic Club that the private passenger car is "the last great freedom."

Detroit abandons air bag research after the Reagan administration repeals passive restraint regulations.

Because the presidential Lincoln limousine is armor plated, assassin John Hinckley's bullet ricochets off its side into President Reagan, severely wounding him.

Suburban home ownership subsidies (property tax and mortgage interest deductions) in the U.S. income tax cost the government $35 billion.

West Edmonton Mall, Canada, the largest in the world with 5.2 billion square feet, costing $1.1 billion, opens. It includes an amusement park, miniature golf course, and 100-meter swimming pool with wave machine. The parking lot holds 30,000 cars.

Wyoming and Louisiana have the highest traffic fatality rates, Massachusetts and Rhode Island the lowest, in the United States.

Of 1,800 drunk drivers convicted in Idaho, only two go to jail.

Students Against Drunk Driving (SADD) founded in Wayland, Massachuetts, High School. Within 10 years it has over four million members.

Statistical analysis suggests that auto fatalities increase by 30 percent in the three days following highly publicized suicides in U.S. cities.

Despite two national championships in the previous four years, Shirley Muldowney cannot find a corporate sponsor, almost certainly because of her gender.

U.S. share of the world auto market slips below 30 percent.

Japan's trade surplus with the United States surpasses $17.6 billion for cars and parts alone.

New U.S. cars produce about 40 percent of their 1960 carbon monoxide levels. G.M. and Chrysler have placed electronic microprocessors on production cars to improve fuel consumption and emissions.

Hudson's, Detroit's largest retailer, closes its downtown store.

G.M. adds market polling and advertising specialists to its design teams. It even hires an outside designer, Pininfarina, whose Cadillac Atlanté fails to sell.

G.M. introduces the "J" cars, a watered-down, underpowered imitation of the Japanese imports, described by auto critic Brock Yates as a "$5 billion blunder." G.M. recalls 245,000.

G.M. levels a Polish neighborhood in Detroit for a new factory, stirring massive controversy.

U.S. firms lay off 291,000 auto workers.

In *Road Warrior*, a postnuclear holocaust, car chase film, Mel Gibson's car features a toilet seat grille.

Twenty millionth VW Beetle produced in Pueblo, Mexico—no longer sold in the United States where it cannot meet safety or air quality standards.

New management team salvages Jaguar.

Pope John Paul II nearly killed by a Bulgarian assassin during a Vatican motorcade. This leads to the creation of the glassed-in, bullet proof "Popemobile."

Fiat produces ethanol-fueled cars in Brazil.

Reagan administration seeks to halt the export of technology to build the Siberian-Western Europe pipeline. The European allies of the United States favor it, hoping to reduce their fuel dependence on Arabs and on U.S. companies.

U.S. Steel buys Marathon Oil, a huge mistake because oil prices plunge in the 1980s.

1982

Ford Escort is the best-selling car in world.

Persons per car: United States—1.8; West Germany—2.7; Italy—2.9; United Kingdom—3.4; France—3.7; Brazil—13.0; U.S.S.R.—27.0; China—14,402.

Most truck trips in the United States are for personal travel, as pickup trucks become fashionable.

Prince becomes one of the first black singers to appear on MTV with his music video, "Little Red Corvette."

Princess Grace of Monaco turns down a chauffeur's offer to take her to town, drives her Rover 3500 through the guardrail on a mountain road, without braking, and dies.

In the United States 71 percent of traffic fatalities are occupants of cars, in Japan only 37 percent.

U.S. Congress creates the computerized National Driver Registry to track traffic law violators from state to state.

Imported autos control 28 percent of the U.S. market.

Only 25,000 car dealers in the United States, down from 45,000 in 1945.

Chrysler begins production of the Hum-Vee, military replacement for the jeep.

Chrysler sells its tank-building subsidiary.

Brazilian-made carburetors on G.M.'s new "J" cars fail with the coming of cold weather. Dealers must replace the defective parts.

UAW gives G.M. $2.4 billion in wage concessions. G.M. president Roger Smith announces that as his contribution he will cut his $9,480 a week salary by $135.

Ford opens an assembly plant in Chihuahua, starting a car-making boom in northern Mexico that will include G.M., Nissan and Chrysler.

Motor vehicle and related industries account for nearly 20 percent of the jobs in the United States.

First Detroit Grand Prix—no U.S. cars entered.

Folkloric rumors of "hippies" in vans dispensing free drugs to elementary school children trigger local scares all over the United States.

Studies show that Japanese cars are less crashworthy than American ones because occupants of small cars are eight times more likely to be killed in crashes than occupants of large cars.

Honda opens an assembly plant in Marysville, Ohio.

Average car age in the United States is 7.2 years, up from 5.7 in 1973. Sweden: 16.2 years. American cars have improved and some consumers may be getting tired of the new car hype.

Britain falls to eighth place in passenger car production, behind even Spain and the USSR.

General Motors shifts European engine production from England to Austria.

Mercedes-Benz makes air bags standard equipment.

Gross profit on a Cadillac: $700; on a Mercedes sold in the United States: $5,000.

Peugeot offers voice advice technologies.

French National Auto Museum based on the old Schlumpf collection opens in Mulhouse. Of its 500 vehicles, 100 are Bugattis and only two are American made. One antique car expert describes the collection as a "nouveau riche extravaganza with no message."

Non-OPEC oil production surpasses OPEC, which begins to cut prices to keep market share and revenue levels.

Reagan administration ends alternative energy programs and oil price controls as the United States reduces its dependence on imported oil to 28 percent of its needs, largely because of more fuel efficient cars.

Exxon (née Standard Oil-New Jersey) centennial—65,000 stations worldwide, six million customers daily, over $62 billion in assets.

Occidental buys Citgo, becomes the eighth largest U.S. oil company.

1983

Of U.S. families with annual incomes over $40,000, half own three or more cars.

Chrysler pays back its government loan, announces record profits.

National Research Council study shows that the 88-kph speed limit saves between 2,000 and 4,000 lives a year, reducing the *rate* of fatal accidents. The study shows that 76 percent of drivers favor the limit, in principle, but 74 percent of rural drivers break it routinely.

U.S. Supreme Court rules DOT cannot abandon passive restraint rules.

California's Bureau of Vehicle Safety inspects 24,721 trucks—74 percent have safety defects, including 32 percent ordered out of service because of severe defects, primarily bad brakes; 36 percent are overweight.

U.S. Justice Department seeks a $4 million fine and recall of G.M. "X" cars, claiming that G.M. concealed a defect that caused at least 13 fatalities and many accidents.

Environmental Pollution Agency reports a significant increase in global warming (the greenhouse effect) caused by fuel emissions, mostly auto-generated carbon dioxide. Cars release 19 pounds of carbon dioxide for every gallon of gas consumed.

U.S. Department of Transportation (DOT) study shows Americans take fewer than 2.5 percent of all trips by public transportation (one-third of all U.S. transit trips are in New York City). Sixty percent of all trips by U.S. children are in cars (compared to 10 percent for Holland). Mothers in both countries are five times more likely to drive their children than fathers. U.S. fathers average 20,800 kilometers a year in cars; women 9,600, largely because the average journey to work is twice as long for a man. Only 30 percent of women over 70 hold driver's licenses.

Freeway shootings kill 12 in Houston.

Federal Trade Commission approves a joint venture between General Motors and Toyota to build cars in California.

Nissan begins to use its own name, not Datsun, on its exports.

Nissan builds a plant in Tennessee.

Toyota produces its forty millionth car.

Pininfarina designs a sports car for Honda.

Chrysler adopts a Japanese robotic and inventory system in its Windsor, Ontario, plant.

"Knight Rider" TV show features an anthropomorphic, computerized Trans-Am smarter than its driver.

Preservationists save a huge, flashing Citgo gas neon billboard, U.S. Route 1 (Kenmore Square), Boston.

British traffic fatalities decline 25 percent in the first year after a compulsory seat belt law goes into effect. Ninety-five percent of British drivers still wear belts two years later. Less than 50 percent of Americans wear them two years after their states pass mandatory laws.

London adopts the Denver boot.

British government sells the old British Leyland, renamed Austin-Rover, to British Aerospace, underwriting £800 million of debt. Total subsidies to date are more than £2 billion.

Ford leads European sales with 13 percent of market.

Summer weekend traffic on the autobahns has become so bad that a German policeman describes them as "the longest sauna in the world."

Nigeria has the highest traffic fatality rate in the world, 234 per 10,000 vehicles. Auto accidents are the leading cause of death for Nigerians between the ages of 5 and 44.

Nowruz well blowout spills 600,000 tons of oil into the Persian Gulf.

Tanker *Castillo de Beliver* catches fire, releases 250,000 tons of oil near Capetown, South Africa.

Trading in oil futures begins on the New York Mercantile Exchange.

British Petroleum drops $2 billion on the Mubrak offshore (Alaska) oil well, the most expensive dry well in history.

1984

New York becomes the first state to require drivers, front-seat passengers, and children under ten to wear seat belts.

U.S. highway expenditures top $50 billion.

U.S. Supreme Court rules that First Amendment guarantees of free speech protect highway billboards from local regulation.

Lee Iacocca's memoirs sell over a million copies.

First minivans.

Los Angeles Museum of Contemporary Art devotes its opening show to automobiles.

Phillip Johnson's AT&T Headquarters in New York, a skyscraper with an exaggerated classical pediment, marks the triumph of postmodernist architecture derived from roadside commercial buildings. Johnson likes the duck-shaped restaurant.

Southern California Association of Governments estimates regional congestion costs $2 billion a year.

Traffic delays average five hours for every employed person in the United States. Cars burn more than 17 billion gallons of gas while jammed.

Repo Man: the first extraterrestrial car movie.

On "Miami Vice," detective Crockett drives a Ferrari seized in drug raid, his signature car.

Authoritative *MIT Report* blames poor management for the decline of the U.S. auto industry, predicts a 60 percent increase in car output globally by 2000.

Congress allows exemptions to antitrust laws for corporate research and development. Within seven years the Big Three will form 12 research consortia.

General Motors restructures into small car and big car divisions.

G.M. purchases H. Ross Perot's Electronic Data Systems for $2.5 billion. Perot becomes G.M.'s largest stockholder.

Seeking high tech capabilities and diversification, G.M. purchases Hughes Aircraft.

Ford president Phillip Caldwell receives $7.3 million in compensation.

Chrysler LeBaron—claimed to be the first computer-designed car.

Credit card parking meters developed in the United Kingdom.

Hong Kong has a higher auto density than any country in the world, 1,191 per square kilometer.

Only 15 percent of India's population of nearly 800 million has ever ridden in a car. The country has 23 million bikes, 17 million bullock carts, and only 1 million cars.

Brazil devotes six million acres to producing ethanol for cars, driving food prices up.

Soviets export 70 million tons of oil to Western Europe (20% of its imports).

Texaco doubles its crude oil reserves by purchasing Getty Oil for $10.1 billion.

Standard Oil of California (SOCAL) takes over Gulf Oil for $13.2 billion, creating the third largest corporation in the United States.

1985

Typical U.S. car weighs 2,700 pounds, down from 3,800 in 1975. The auto industry now puts more aluminum and plastic in cars than cast iron. More than 10 percent of the weight of new cars is plastic. Average fuel economy has nearly doubled, but is still lowest in world.

Brookings Institution study convinces the Reagan administration to relax CAFE standards, arguing that the marketplace, not regulation, led to increased fuel efficiency in 1970s.

Smithsonian Institute's Museum of American History runs an exhibit on the evolution of the motel.

Over 5,000 Kentucky Fried Chicken franchises in the United States.

In the United States over 155,400 square kilometers are paved.

Jim Pattison buys John Lennon's psychedelically painted Rolls-Royce for $2,229,000.

Insurance Institute reports that dealers sell the parts needed to make a $10,500 Chevrolet for $37,600 *plus labor*.

New Jersey study suggests mandatory jail terms for drunk driving are counterproductive because juries are more reluctant to convict drunk drivers and hit and run accidents become more common.

Colorado reports that 17 percent of car owners in inspected areas and 31 percent in uninspected areas have tampered with their pollution control systems.

Etak Company introduces a primitive car navigational computer.

Honda surpasses Nissan and Toyota in U.S. sales, A.M.C. in U.S. production.

Chevrolet and Toyota (the primary owner) begin joint production of Novas in California.

G.M. locates the plant for its new car division, Saturn, in Tennessee. Saturns will not hit the market for six years.

After a lengthy political battle, New York City decides not to build the Westway, largely for environmental reasons.

New Jersey Turnpike installs a computerized traffic monitoring and control system with the ability to flash warning signs, adjust speed limits and close exits.

Auto accidents kill 200,000 people worldwide.

Toyota's Land Cruiser is the world's top-selling four-wheel drive vehicle.

Nissan agrees to build a British factory to escape the U.K.'s 11 percent import quota.

Korea produces more than one million cars.

Hong Kong experiments with electronic road pricing.

Saudis decide to flood world oil markets, dropping prices to a half of 1983 levels.

World oil consumption down to 52 million barrels per day, a 20 percent decline in six years.

OPEC share of world oil production is 28 percent, down from over 50 percent in 1979.

1986

Centennial of the i.c. automobile.

Only New York City and Chicago have more corporate headquarters in the United States than Connecticut's suburban Fairfield County. Of the 128 corporate headquarters in Manhattan in 1965, only 53 remain.

Los Angeles plans a subway system, hoping to create a rail-based central city on the nineteenth-century model to relieve freeway congestion.

Lead emissions in United States are down 94 percent from peak, but only 5 percent of the gas sold in Western Europe is unleaded.

U.S. government collects $147 million in gas guzzler taxes of at least $500 on cars getting less than 22.5 mpg (9.6 kpl).

University of Massachusetts Medical Center study shows that smokers are 50 percent more likely to have auto accidents than nonsmokers.

MADD helps spread the urban folk tale about the drunk who wakes up the morning after a bender to find a dead child impaled on his car's grille.

California requires those convicted of drunk driving to install breathalyzer interlocks on their cars.

Congress requires states to increase the drinking age to 21 as a precondition for federal highway aid.

Nebraska, Massachusetts and New York voters repeal mandatory seat belt laws in referenda.

Motor Trend describes the Cadillac Eldorado as the worst car of the year. G.M. can only sell them with a $9,000 rebate.

Ford, now clearly the styling leader among U.S. firms, surpasses G.M. in profits for first time since 1924. Its European-designed Escort and Taurus models lead the way.

Ford sets up an Auto Safety Office, which seeks to improve design by litigation review.

H. Ross Perot criticizes G.M. management as overpaid and out of touch with both customers and workers. G.M. buys Perot out for a $741 million profit, conditional on his ceasing to criticize G.M. management openly.

G.M. introduces Japanese systems in a Buick factory in Flint, Michigan.

G.M. buys the British sports car firm, Lotus.

Beverly Hills's Tony Thompson, the top-selling Rolls-Royce dealer in the world, who sells over 100 cars a year, reports: "In America and particularly on the West Coast, no stigma is attached to overt displays of wealth."

More than 85 percent of new cars in the United States have air conditioning and automatic transmissions. Over 40 percent have stereos. All reduce fuel efficiency.

Hyundai (Korea) begins to export cars to the United States.

Terrorists assassinate Georges Bessy, president of Renault, who had laid off 45,000 workers.

The Volkswagen Golf is now the best-selling car in Europe. Volkswagen purchases the Spanish company SEAT.

German proverb: "A man who drives a Porsche is a man with his fly undone."

German cities have more than 800 traffic-free zones.

London's ring road, supposedly the longest beltway at 185.2 kilometers, completed after 14 years at a cost of £1 billion. Traffic jams it on its first day.

Western European oil consumption down to 75 percent of 1972 levels.

Crude oil prices fall by a third—not reflected at the gas pump.

1987

U.S. Congress gives states the right to increase speed limits to 104 kph (65 mph) on rural sections of interstates. Within two years auto fatalities on those roads will go up 31 percent.

Travel times have declined 20 percent in five years in Los Angeles, San Francisco, Washington, D.C., and Atlanta since 1982.

DOT requires passive restraints by 1990. This time it will stick.

Hot Rod Magazine publishes its first swimsuit issue.

Big Three deploy 26,000 industrial robots, but still cannot come close to Japanese productivity.

Sayanora A.M.C. Chrysler purchases the remnants from Renault.

Tolls per kilometer on turnpikes: Delaware—13.8¢; New Hampshire—9.0¢; West Virginia—7.4¢; Massachusetts—6.5¢; Pennsylvania—6.4¢; New Jersey—6.2¢; New York—4.9¢; Maine—4.6¢.

Critics of Detroit's new subway point out that fares will only cover 20 percent of operating costs. The *Detroit News* complains that the $210 million spent on construction could have purchased 11,000 buses and 12,000 handi-vans, as well as a subcompact car for every carless family in Detroit.

Seventy freeway shootings terrify Los Angeles.

In rapidly developing Orange County, outside Los Angeles, traffic has increased by a factor of fifty in the previous ten years. Half the residents believe that it is the most important political problem in the county.

Lincoln becomes the first U.S. firm to offer CD players.

Ford buys Aston-Martin.

Rolls-Royce offers the Phantom VI limousine for £195,595.

Margaret Thatcher's British government privatizes Rolls-Royce.

Fiat, which now has the highest worker productivity in Europe (double its 1977 levels), purchases Alfa-Romeo, quashes its collaboration with Nissan.

Pininfarina-built Cadillac Atlanté bodies flown from Italy to the United States.

Christie's auctions a 1931 Bugatti Royale for $9,845,000, the highest price ever paid for a car.

Tierra Del Fuego-Point Barrow trip takes 24 days with a short sea ride off Panama to bypass a road gap.

Suzuki buys the old Murati plant, agrees to produce 100,000 cars a year in India.

1988

Southern California Association of Governments forecasts daytime 24-kph average speed on the freeways by 2000.

Henry Ford Museum sets up an exhibit of 1940s roadside architecture.

American junkyards contain an estimated two to three billion abandoned tires.

Surveys show 80 percent of drivers whose licenses have been revoked continue to drive, but they have 72 percent fewer accidents than other drivers.

Drunk driver Larry Mahoney, cruising down I-71 in Kentucky on the wrong side of the road, hits a school bus head-on, killing 23 children and 6 adults, likely the worst accident in U.S. history.

Most U.S. states report a more than 1,000 percent increase in liability insurance for taverns since 1980 as courts increasingly hold them responsible for accidents caused by drunken customers.

G.M. drops its expectations dramatically, seeking only a 36 percent U.S. market share.

G.M. makes record profits, primarily because of its European operations.

G.M. president Roger Smith lays off 42,000 workers, receives $3.7 million in profitsharing.

Typical new cars around the world now contain over 200 pounds of plastic.

Leading exporter of cars made in the United States—Honda, which even exports some U.S.-made cars to Japan.

Britain's Ministry of Transport commissions a study of German "traffic-calming" techniques, that try to slow down the speed of cars in residential neighborhoods, not by largely unenforceable speed limits, but by design techniques like narrowing streets, chicanes, raised pedestrian crossings, and speed bumps.

Ford's English factories have doubled productivity in eight years, but it still is 25 percent lower than Ford's German plants.

Volkswagen shuts its U.S. factory.

Honda begins to export cars from the United States to Japan.

Benz agrees to pay any of its World War II slave laborers who are still alive.

Jaguar production cars claim a road speed of 328 kph.

World Bank loans for urban transport from 1972 to 1988 in Asia went 68 percent for roads, only 14 percent for public transport.

Explosion of an Occidental Petroleum North Sea rig kills 166 workers.

1989

Thirty-eight years after they were patented, Chrysler announces that it will put air bags in all new cars. Ford follows suit. Both only provide driver side air bags.

During the Reagan years, the National Highway and Traffic Safety Administration has not issued a single new rule.

Congress approves the new Clean Air Act that encourages states to require alternative automotive fuels.

Of the nine makes of cars with the highest consumer satisfaction records in the United States, six are Japanese and two are West German.

As requested in her will, heirs bury small town Indiana resident Aurora Shuck with her 1976 Cadillac.

Mourners bury murdered Detroit drug lord "Maserati" Rick Carter in a casket made from a Mercedes.

Encyclopedia of Southern Culture claims that half the family vehicles in the south are pickup trucks, the leading symbol of southern masculinity.

American Medical Association estimates the health costs of air pollution at $40 to $50 billion per year.

Volkswagen Beetle begins its 50th production year, now only produced in Mexico. It can no longer be sold in the United States, because it cannot meet safety or emission standards.

Ford has the most productive North American factories, outpacing even Japanese-owned, nonunion plants. Top quality is achieved in Hermosillo, Mexico.

Despite investing $67 billion in plants in the 1980s, G.M. has the lowest levels of productivity.

Roger and Me, a popular documentary film, attacks Roger Smith and G.M. for callously destroying the economy of Flint, Michigan.

Nissan workers in a Tennessee factory vote down the UAW by a two to one margin.

Top-selling U.S.-made model in United States—Honda Accord.

Goodyear becomes the last American-owned major tire producer after Michelin purchases Uniroyal-Goodrich. A German firm has recently bought General Tire and a Japanese firm Firestone.

Insurance Industry Research Council rates Boston drivers the worst in the nation with an accident rate 63 percent higher than New York City drivers, the second worst.

I-95 bridge, Greenwich, Connecticut, collapses, suggesting major maintenance problems with the interstate system.

After a traffic dispute, 52-year-old Wall Street banker Arthur Solomon gets out of his Mercedes and shoots a college student.

Federal Communications Commission authorizes radio beacon antitheft devices.

Los Angeles Times survey shows that 5 percent of L.A. drivers admit that they are carrying handguns.

During the World Series earthquake, the elevated Nimitz Freeway in Oakland and several lanes of the Golden Gate Bridge collapse.

All major U.S. and Japanese firms and Volvo have located their advanced concept styling centers in Southern California.

General Motors buys 50 percent of Saab.

Ford purchases Jaguar, the last British-owned auto maker.

Prime Minister Thatcher convinces Toyota to locate a plant in Britain. Honda acquires 20 percent of Austin-Rover. The Japanese plan to enter the continental market in 1992 when European tariff barriers come down.

London commuters experience a 53-kilometer-long traffic jam. Rio de Janeiro and Seoul police estimate that the "rush hour" now lasts 14 hours.

Germany's parliament retains unlimited speed on the autobahns, after one member declares it a national treasure that encourages engineering excellence.

Soviet Union suffers 60,000 traffic fatalities, 10 times the Western European rate.

Hyundai opens a factory in Quebec.

Boston physician notes that the leading cause of death for U.S. tourists in the third world is auto accidents.

Chrysler wins the contract to build China's first car factory.

Mexico moves toward free trade in cars, significantly lowering local content rules.

Largely because of cars, East Asia's inter-regional trade is higher than its extra-regional trade for the first time since World War II.

Exxon Valdez grounding spills 11.2 million gallons of oil into Prince William Sound, Alaska. Exxon claims that its ineffective clean-up cost $2.6 billion.

Bush administration announces that methanol will be at the heart of its fuels/air pollution policies.

1990

Cultural critic O. B. Hardison writes: "In antiquity, temple architecture and religious sculpture were complementary. . . . A temple was planned for the statue of a god. . . . A similar relationship links modern dual lane highways with the most popular three dimensional art form ever created, the thin steel sculpture known as the automobile."

Toyota becomes the world's largest car maker.

Korean and Brazilian car sales in the United States plunge 50 percent, largely because of quality problems.

Roger Smith retires from G.M. after 11 years as president. During his regime, G.M. has lost 25 percent of its U.S. market share.

Hollywood revives the 1960s macho car-racing genre of movie as Tom Cruise stars in *Days of Thunder*.

Deaths per 10,000 cars in United States—Best: Audi 5000, Cadillac Fleetwood, Chevrolet Cavalier station wagon, Olds Cutlass station wagon, and Toyota Cressida—all 1.1. Worst: Corvette—5.2, Camaro—5.9, Dodge Charger—4.5, Ford Mustang—4.4, and Nissan 300ZX—4.2. This primarily reflects the sort of person who drives the cars.

Chrysler becomes the first U.S. car company to offer air bags as standard equipment, 37 years after the first air bag patent. Lee Iacocca, once an opponent, now pushes them.

In the first head-on collision of air-bagged cars, two drivers walk away from an accident in Culpeper, Virginia.

U.S. Supreme Court rules that random roadside sobriety checks are legal.

Typical U.S. household has twice as many cars as children.

Millions of I-5 (California) motorists drive by Juan Francisco Camacho, who lies unconscious at the roadside for four days after a hit-and-run accident.

More than half of Americans live in metropolitan areas that violate the EPA's safety standard for ozone.

President Bush signs an extension of the Clean Air Act with some provisions stricter than its predecessor, but successfully lobbies Congress to avoid new fuel economy standards for cars.

Paris mayor Jacques Chirac announces plans to eliminate 100,000 downtown parking spots.

Volkswagen ad in Italy: "The car to buy, if you want to beat the Germans to the beach."

Mexico passes a clean air law, banning leaded gasoline and limiting Mexico City car owners by mandating that even- and odd-numbered license plates may only be on the road on alternate days.

Fifty Saudi women protest the law banning women drivers by driving in Riyadh. The Islamic morality police suggest their execution.

Japan's half million auto workers produce ten million cars, 70 times the productivity of China's 1.6 million workers, who produce only a half million cars.

Worker hours per car: Japan—16.8; North America—24.9; Western Europe—35.8; U.S.S.R.—120.

Soviet oil embargo temporarily blunts Lithuanian independence moves.

Consumers now pump 80 percent of the gasoline sold in the United States.

By midsummer the United States is importing over 50 percent of its oil needs, exceeding even early 1970s import rates.

Bangkok plans a rapid transit system to relieve traffic jams.

Iraqi overthrow of the Kuwait government leads to another oil crisis. President Bush defends the dispatch of American troops because cheap oil is "essential to the American way of life."

1991

The United States and the allies defeat Iraq. Huge oil spills in the Persian Gulf are a byproduct of the war. Kuwait faces massive air pollution from oil wells set afire by the retreating Iraqis.

Michigan Chronicle coins a new word: "carjack," a crime that seems to be on the increase because of improved antitheft measures. Detroit and Washington, D.C., lead the way.

Comprehensive analysis of mandatory-sentencing DWI laws passed in the last 20 years by Britain, France, Washington, Tennessee, and California show only a short-run reduction in drunk driving.

Florida police arrest Aileen Wournos, the first woman serial killer, who has killed at least 14 middle-aged men at highway rest stops.

Over 16 million visitors stop at the Oceanside California, rest stop, the busiest in the United States.

California Air Resources Board requires that car makers must market at least 2 percent of their sales as "zero emissions" (i.e. electric) vehicles by 1998, 10 percent by 2003.

J. D. Powers Survey shows that only 14 percent of Americans over 65 drive foreign cars, but 46 percent of those aged 25 to 34 do so.

New York City police tow over 100,000 illegally parked cars.

Second Annual International Conference on Car Free Cities attracts 1,500 people.

Since 1983 the mileage driven by American women has quadrupled, largely because more married women are working and commuting.

Hollywood releases *Class Action*, a courtroom docudrama based on the exploding Pinto gas tanks of the 1970s.

Film *Thelma and Louise* recapitulates the Odyssey theme, but with women as the warriors on the road in a Ford Thunderbird.

Robin Williams stars as a hyperactive car salesperson in the film *Cadillac Man*.

Simon and Schuster starts the Tom Swift III Series with *The Black Dragon*, in which Swift invents a flying skateboard.

After five years Porsche 911 retains 79 percent of its value, based on resale prices, Yugos only 25 percent, the best and worst resale values of cars sold in the United States.

Democratic presidential hopefuls attack G.M. for laying off 74,000 workers while paying Roger Smith a $1.2 million annual pension.

G.M. loses $4.5 billion, the largest corporate deficit ever.

G.M. considers selling its 34 percent share in Isuzu, which has led to few cooperative projects, after Isuzu posts a $381 million loss.

Ford's 25 percent share of Mazda has produced new markets for Mazda; quality awards for jointly built Escorts, Navahos and Probes; and a dealer network that makes Ford the largest Japanese import.

As the value of the dollar declines, Peugeot and Sterling pull out of the American market.

Global bicycle production up 40 percent (to 100 million) in the last 20 years. Over 800 million people own bikes, compared to 460 million cars. The growth is largely a product of the Chinese economic revolution that has put bike ownership within reach of many.

Japan's Akashi Strait Bridge spans 1,780 meters.

Soichiro Honda dies.

South Korean military agrees to use its helicopters to pluck disabled cars out of Seoul's massive traffic jams.

Britain's largest car manufacturer: Nissan.

1992

Traffic fatalities decline by 8 percent, the largest peacetime decrease ever, as only 39,235 Americans die on the road. Reasons for the decline include more seat belt use, less drunken driving, an aging population, and a reduction in the number of trips because of a recession.

Sober drivers are more likely to kill drunk pedestrians than drunk drivers sober pedestrians.

Most heavily traveled roads in United States—Hawaii, New Jersey and California.

Federal Highway Commission reports that more than 35 percent of interstate highways in Missouri, Alaska, North Dakota, and Oregon need repair; less than 1 percent in South Dakota Hawaii, Delaware, and Alabama.

Busiest stretches of interstate highway and daily volumes: I-95 (George Washington Bridge in New York City)—249,300; I-90 (Dan Ryan Expressway, Chicago)—248,000; I-10 (San Bernardino Freeway, Los Angeles)—224,000; I-5 (Seattle)—224,000.

Newark leads the United States in car thefts with a rate of 5 per 100,000 population. Most thieves are joy-riding adolescents, including an 11-year-old whom the police have caught 15 times.

Victor Gruen designs the largest mall in the United States, the Mall of America, in Bloomington, Minnesota, with 400 stores and 13,000 parking spots. On 658 acres, costing $650 million to build, it includes a roller coaster, a four-story waterfall, 300 trees, and 30,000 plants. The mall centers on a forty-foot-high inflatable Snoopy (the god of consumerism?).

Ford Taurus, with the "jellybean" look, replaces the Honda Accord as the top-selling U.S. model.

J. D. Powers Survey shows that 46 percent of U.S. cars have women as their principal drivers. Most driven are Geo Storm—74 percent; Isuzu I-Mark—74 percent; and Nissan Pulsar—71 percent. The cars most likely to be driven by men are Ferrari—100 percent; Acura NSX—96 percent; Volvo 780—91 percent; and BMW 6 Series—88 percent. Women consumers say that they are most concerned with operating costs and safety. Eighty-four percent want dual air bags. Women now buy 49 percent of all cars, up from 37 percent in 1991.

Ford agrees to one price marketing of the Escort, after surveys show that minorities and women pay more for new cars.

Los Angeles Rapid Transit District puts barrel-shaped benches at bus stops, impossible for homeless people to sleep on.

Sixteen-kilometer commutes in Los Angeles average 35 minutes, compared to 20 minutes in 1980.

Los Angeles subway opens.

Los Angeles Drive Me Wild exhibition features sculptures of rush hour drivers stalled in their cars.

In seven U.S. cities, led by Oklahoma City, more than 90 percent of households have two cars. In five cities more than 20 percent of households (led by New York at 36 percent) have no car.

Presidents of the Big Three accompany President Bush to Japan, after they accuse Mazda and Toyota of dumping.

G.M. is spending $929 per vehicle on employee health insurance, compared to $529 for Ford.

G.M.'s board of directors fires President Robert C. Stempel as its market share continues to shrink.

Ford gives major promotions to executives Edsel Ford II and William Clay Ford, Jr., great-grandsons of Henry.

Chevrolet paints the one millionth Corvette "Arrest Me Red."

Thieves steal a kilometer of guard rail from the Chicago Skyway.

Florida roadside attraction: Tragedy in U.S. History Museum.

Elvis Presley Auto Museum opens.

Red Sox player Jack Clark files for bankruptcy despite his seven-figure salary, largely because he has spent $1.7 million on 18 cars, including 5 1950s muscle cars, 3 Mercedes, 2 Ferraris, and 3 G.M. vans.

Motor Trend Magazine reports that the Corvette has the best acceleration time (0 to 100 kph in 4.4 seconds) and the best breaking distance (100 kph to 0 in 32.7 meters) of any make. The Suzuki Sidekick has the slowest 0 to 100 kph acceleration time (15.8 seconds).

NBC News program "Dateline" charges that G.M. has deliberately sold pickup trucks with unsafe gas tanks because redesign would be too expensive. G.M. will sue NBC, because the truck explosion viewed in the show was rigged.

Big Three representatives expel Honda from the Motor Vehicle Manufacturer's Association, change its name back to the American Automobile Manufacturer's Association.

Japanese car makers face declining profits because of unfavorable exchange rates and the global recession.

Toyota begins to export U.S.-made Camrys to Japan in large numbers and is turning out some right hand drive models in the United States for export to Britain.

Mexico City, which had 192 smog alert days in 1991, experiences its worst smog alert with ozone levels four times the dangerous level. The city closes all schools and factories for the duration of the crisis and bans half its motor vehicles daily.

Striking French truckers barricade Paris with their vehicles.

Half a million visitors tour the French National Auto Museum, the third most popular museum in France, despite its location in remote Mulhouse.

In the five years since the beginning of the Intifada, many more Israelis have lost their lives in auto accidents than to Palestinian violence.

For the first time, more than a million motor vehicles are sold in China, a 50 percent increase over 1991.

1993

G.M. announces a 1992 loss of $23 billion, the largest ever for any corporation.

Ford offers roadside service on all cars.

NHTSA estimates that motorized seat belts are saving 5,300 lives a year and even air bags, which relatively few cars have, are saving 2,400 lives a year.

More than 54 million Americans are living in counties that fail to meet national clean air standards.

Suicide doctor Jack Kervorkian notes that carbon monoxide emissions from cars are now too low for suicidal owners.

Chevrolet introduces its new Camaro muscle car: "What else would you expect from the country that invented rock and roll?"

New York's Museum of Modern Art opens its exhibit, Designed for Speed, Three Automobiles by Ferrari. The Museum adds a 1990 Ferrari 641 racer to its collection.

Over 500 carjackings in Atlanta. Suburbanites see the increase as marking the spread of urban crime to the suburbs.

Florida governor Chiles orders armed guards at interstate rest stops after carjackers slay nine European tourists.

Over 300 U.S. cities have some police bicycle patrols.

Insurance Institute for Highway Safety Studies show that airbags reduce the risk of a fatal injury by 23 percent and serious injury by 68 percent.

G.M. sells Lotus to Bugatti.

Volkswagen loses DM 1.26 million in the first quarter. Ferdinand Porsche's nephew, Ferdinand Pieche, becomes president of the firm.

Germany announces plans to privatize the autobahns. Profits from the sale to a toll-collecting firm will be used to upgrade Germany's rail system.

1994

O. J. Simpson car chase.

Los Angeles earthquake collapses two major freeway overpasses.

Seattle reports traffic up 120 percent in previous 10 years.

Federal highway officials predict a quadrupling of highway congestion over the next 20 years.

Surveys in the traffic-choked downtown neighborhoods of four different major cities show childhood asthma rates more than double the national average.

Sally Field drives a Volvo, the symbol of suburban safety consciousness, in *Mrs. Doubtfire*.

Imports are 14 percent of the U.S. market, down from 22 percent in 1991. U.S. car firms have the lowest cost per car in the world.

Oldsmobile introduces an on-board navigation system.

Volvo introduces side impact air bags.

Appendix A: Tables

Table A.1
Ford and Cadillac Prices, 1900–1990

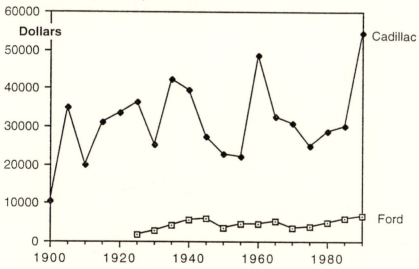

Table A.2
Ford and Cadillac Horsepower, 1900–1990

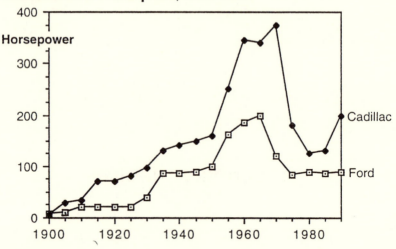

Table A.3
Ford, Toyota and Volkswagen Horsepower, 1960–1990

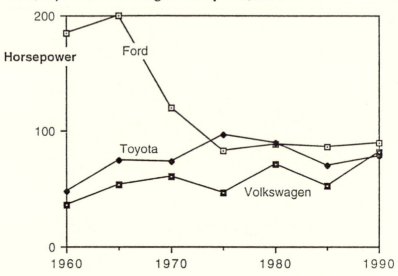

Table A.4
Sales by Detroit's Big Three Automakers, 1910–1990

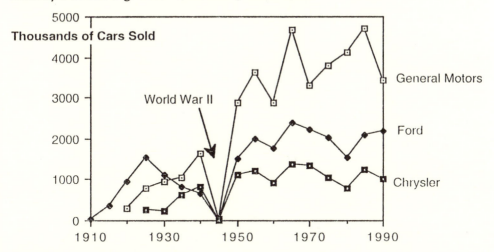

Table A.5
Share of the U.S. Market, by Firm, 1915–1990

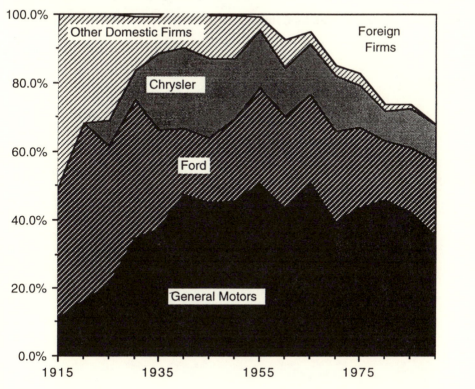

Table A.6
European Car Production, by Country, 1920–1940

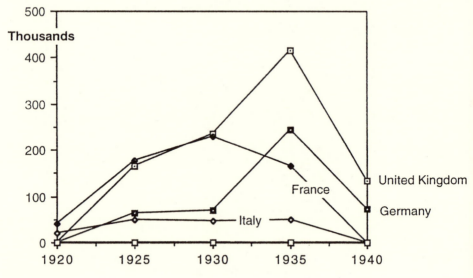

Table A.7
European Car Production, by Country, 1945–1990

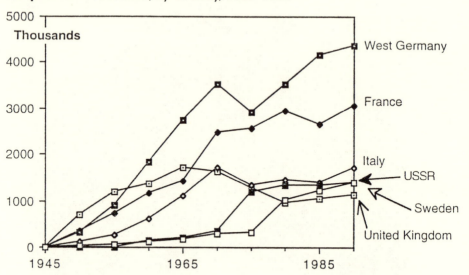

Table A.8
World Oil Consumption, by Continent, 1950–1990

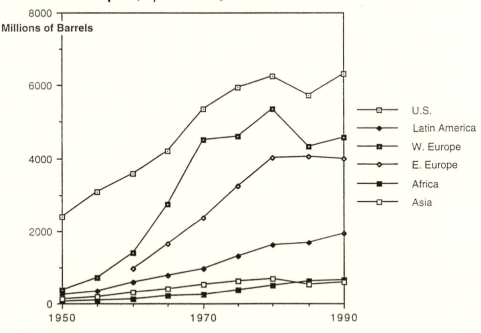

Table A.9
U.S. Gasoline Prices, 1925–1988

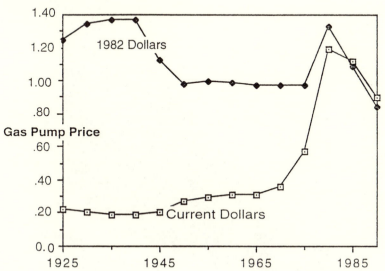

Table A.10
U.S. Petroleum Production and Consumption, 1960–1990

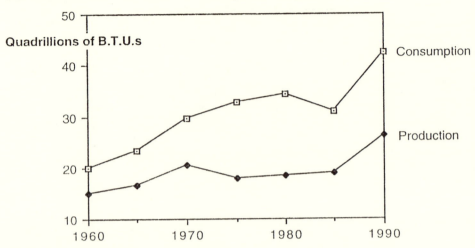

Table A.11
World Auto Registration, 1950–1990

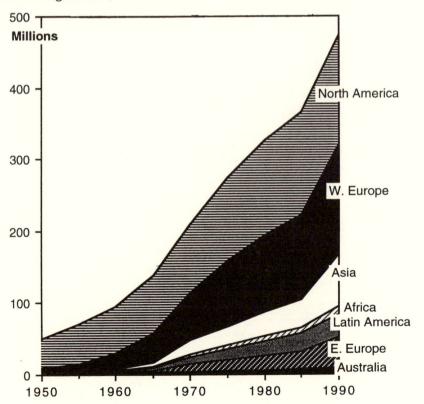

Table A.12
Persons per Car, United States, 1925–1990

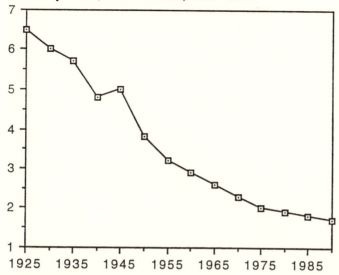

Table A.13
Persons per Car, Selected European Countries, 1930–1960

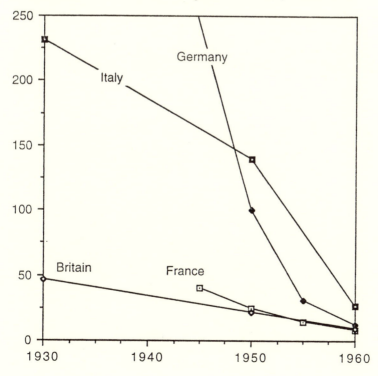

Table A.14
**Persons per Car, Selected European Countries and the United States,
1965–1990**

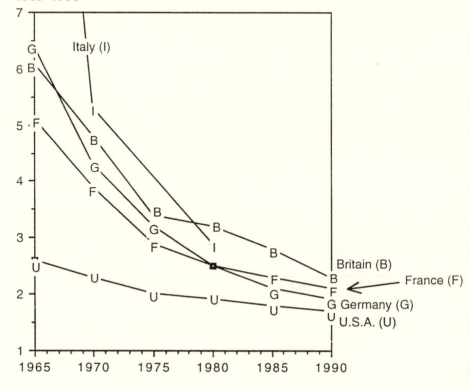

Appendix B: North American Car Museums

Note: A number of these museums are quite small or have unusual opening hours, so check with them before visiting.

ALBERTA, CANADA

Reynolds Museum
4110–57 Street
Wetaskiwin AB T9A 2B6
(403)352–5201

ARKANSAS

The Museum of Automobiles
Route 3, Petit Jean Mountain
Morrilton, AR 72110
(501)727–5427

CALIFORNIA

Blackhawk Automotive Museum
3700 Blackhawk Plaza Circle
Danville, CA 94506
(510) 736–2277

Deer Park Auto Museum
2903 Champagne Blvd.
Escondido, CA 92026
(619)749–1666

Dennis Mitosinka's Classic Cars
619 E. Fourth Street
Santa Ana, CA 92701
(714)953–5303

Ed Cholakian All Cadillacs of the 40s
12811 Champagne Blvd.
Sylmar, CA 91342
(818)361–1147

The Nethercut Collection
15180 Bledsoe Street
Sylmar, CA 91342
(818)367–1085

The Petersen Automotive Museum
6060 Wilshire Blvd.
Los Angeles, CA 90036
(213)964–6356

Reggie Jackson's Performance Cars & Baseball Memorabilia
3700 Blackhawk Plaza Circle
Danville, CA 94506
(510)736–2280 ext. 248

Route 66 Territory Visitors Center & Museum
Thomas Winery Plaza
7965 Vineyard Avenue/Suite F5
Rancho Cucamonga, CA 91730
(909)948–9166

The San Diego Automotive Museum
2080 Pan American
Balboa Park
San Diego, CA 92101
(619)231–2886

San Francisco Maritime National History Park
2905 Hyde Street
San Francisco, CA 94109
(415)556–3002

Specialty Sales
4321 First Street
Pleasanton, CA 94566
(800)600–2262
(818)361–1147

Towe Ford Museum
220 Front Street
Sacramento, CA 95818
(916)442–6802

Vintage Coach Museum
16593 Arrow Blvd.
Fontana, CA 92335
(909)823–9168

Vintage Museum of Transport
1421 Emerson Avenuye
Oxnard, CA 93033
(805)486–5929

COLORADO

Doughtery Museum
8306 N. 107th Street/US 287
Longmont, CO 80501
(303)776–2520

Forney Transportation Museum
1416 Platt Street
Denver, CO 80202
(303)433–5896

Ghost Town
400 S. 21st Street
Corner of Highway 24W & 21st Street
Colorado Springs, CO 80907
(719)634–2520

CONNECTICUT

Hartford Automobile Club
815 Farmington Avenue
West Hartford, CT 06119
(203)236–3261

DISTRICT OF COLUMBIA

National Museum of American History
14th Street of Constitution
Washington, DC 20560
(202)357–2700

FLORIDA

Bellm Cars & Music of Yesterday
5500 North Tamiami Trail
Sarasota, FL 34243
(941)355–6228

Don Garlits Museum of Drag Racing
13700 South West 16th Avenue
Ocala, FL 32676
(904)245–8661

Elliott Museum
825 NE Ocean Blvd.
Hutchinson Island
Stuart, FL 34996
(407)225–1961

Silver Springs Antique Car Collection
5656 E. Silver Springs Blvd.
P.O. Box 370
Silver Springs, FL 32688
(904)236–2121

GEORGIA

Museo Abarth
1111 Via Bayless
Marietta, GA 30066–2770
(404)928–1446

Old Car City U.S.A.
3098 Highway 411 NE
P.O. Box 480
White, GA 30184
(404)382–6141

IDAHO

Vintage Car Museum
218 Cedar Street
Sandpoint, ID 83864
(208)263–7173

ILLINOIS

Grant Hills Antique Auto Museum
Route 20 East
Galena, IL 61036
(815)777–2115

Hartung's License Plate and Auto Museum
3623 West Lake Street
Glenview, IL 60025
(708)724–4354

Museum of Science and Industry
57th Street and Lakeshore Drive
Chicago, IL 60637
(312)684–1414

Volo Antique Auto Museum
27640 W. Highway 120
Volo, Il 60073
(815)385–3644

INDIANA

Auburn-Cord-Duesenberg Museum
1600 S. Wayne Street
P.O. Box 271
Auburn, IN 46706
(219)925–1444

Elmwood Haynes Museum
1915 South Webster Street
Kokomo, IN 46902–2040
(317)456–2500

Indianapolis Motor Speedway Hall of Fame Museum
4790 W. 16th Street
Indianapolis, IN 46222
(317)484–6747

S. Ray Miller Antique Auto Museum
2130 Middlebury Street
Elkhart, IN 46516
(219)522–0539

Studebaker National Museum
525 S. Main Street
South Bend, IN 46601
(219)235–9714

IOWA

Iowa State Historical Museum
East 12th and Grand Avenue
Des Moines, IA 50319
(515)281–8788

National Spring Car Hall of Fame
One Sprint Capital Place
P.O. Box 542
Knoxville, IA 50138–3425
(515)842–6176

Van Horn's Antique Truck Museum
Highway 65 North
Mason City, IA 50401
(515)423–0550

KANSAS

Kansas Museum of History
6425 SW 6th
Topeka, KS 66615
(913)272–8681

KENTUCKY

The National Corvette Museum
2800 Scottsville Road
Bowling Green, KY 42102
(502)781–7973

Rineyville Sandblasting Model A Ford Museum
179 Arvel Wise Lane
Elizabethown, KY 42701
(502)862–4671

MAINE

Boothbay Railway Village
Route 27
P.O. Box 123
Boothbay, ME 04537
(207)633–4727

Cole Land Transportation Museum
405 Perry Road
Bangor, ME 04401
(207)990–3600

Owls Head Transportation Museum
Route 73
P.O. Box 277
Owls Head, ME 04854
(207)594–4418

The Stanley Museum
School Street
P.O. Box 281
Kingfield, ME 04947–0280
(207)265–2729

Wells Auto Museum and Museum
Route 1
P.O. Box 496
Wells, ME 04090
(207)646–9064

MASSACHUSETTS

Heritage Plantation of Sandwich
Pine and Grove Streets
Sandwich, MA 02563
(508)888–3300

Museum of Transportation
125 Newton Street
Larz Anderson Park
Brookline, MA 02146
(617)522–6547

MICHIGAN

Alfred P. Sloan Museum
1221 E. Kearsley Street
Flint, MI 48503
(810)760–1169

Automotive Hall of Fame
3225 Cook Road
P.O. Box 1727
Midland, MI 48641–1727
(517)631–5760

Detroit Historical Museum
5401 Woodward
Detroit, MI 48202
(313)833–1805

Gilmore-CCCA Museum
6965 Hickory Road
Hickory Corners, MI 49060
(616)671–5089

Henry Ford Museum and Greenfield Village
20900 Oakwood Blvd.
P.O. Box 1970
Dearborn, MI 48121
(313)217–1620

R. E. Olds Transportation Museum
240 Museum Drive
Lansing, MI 48933
(517)372–0422

MINNESOTA

Ellingson Car Museum
20950 Rogers Drive
Rogers, MN 55374
(612)252–2080

MISSOURI

Main Street Motor Museum
315 North Main
Independence, MO 64050
(816)252–2080

Memoryville U.S.A. Auto Museum
1008 West 12th Street
Junction of I-44 and Highway 63
Rolla, MO 65401
(314)364–1810

National Museum of Transport
3015 Barretts Station Road
St. Louis, MO 63122
(314)965–7998

Patee House Museum
12th and Penn Streets
P.O. Box 1022
St. Joseph, MO 64503
(813)232–8206

MONTANA

Oscar's Dreamland
3100 Harrow Drive
Billings, MT 59102
(406)656–0966

Towe Ford Museum
Old Montana Prison
1106 Main Street
Deer Lodge, MT 59722
(406)846–3111

NEBRASKA

Chevyland U.S.A. Auto and Cycle Museum
Route 1, I-80, Exit 257
Elm Creek, NE 68836
(308)856–4208

Harold Warp Pioneer Village Foundation
Highways 6 and 34
Minden, NE 68959
(800)445–4447

Hastings Museum
1330 N. Burlington Avenue
Hastings, NE 68901
(402)461–2399

Sawyer's Sandhills Museum
440 Valentine Street
Valentine, NE 69201
(402)376–3293

Stuhr Museum of the Prairie Pioneer
3133 West Highway 34
Highways 34 and 281
Grand Island, NE 68801
(308)385–5316

NEVADA

Imperial Palace Auto Collection
3535 Las Vegas Blvd. South
Las Vegas, NV 89103
(702)731–3311

National Automobile Museum
10 Lake Street South
Reno, NV 89501
(702)333–9300

NEW HAMPSHIRE

Crossroads of America
Route 302 and Trudeau Road
Bethlehem, NH 03574
(603)869–3919

Westminister MG Car Museum
South Street
P.O. Box 37
Walpole, NH 03608–0037

NEW JERSEY

Space Farms Zoo and Museum
218 Route 519 Beemerville
Sussex, NJ 07461
(201)875–5800

NEW YORK

American Museum of Fire Fighting
125 Harry Howard Avenue
Hudson, NY 12534
(518)828–7695 ext. 116

Cole Palen's Old Rhinebeck Aerodome
42 Stone Church Road
Rhinebeck, NY 12572
(914)758–8610

Collectors Cars, Inc.
56 West Merrick Road
Freeport, NY 11520
(516)378–6666

D.I.R.T. Hall of Fame and Classic Car Museum
1 Speedway Drive
P.O. Box 240
Weedsport, NY 13166
(315)834–6667

The Himes Museum of Motor Racing Nostalgia
15 O'Neil Avenue
Bayshore, NY 11706
(516)666–4912

Old Stone Fort Museum Complex
N. Main Street
RD 2, Box 30A
Schoharie, NY 12157
(518)295–7192

NORTH CAROLINA

Backing Up Classics
4545 Highway 29
Harrisburg, NC 28075
(603)756–4121

North Carolina Transportation Museum
411 S. Salisbury Avenue
P.O. Box 165
Spencer, NC 28159
(704)636–2889

Richard Petty Museum
311 Branson Mill Road
Randelman, NC 27317
(910)495–1143

NORTH DAKOTA

Bonanzaville USA
I-94 and US 10
P.O. Box 719
West Fargo, ND 58078
(701)282–2822

OHIO

Allen County Museum
620 West Market Street
Lima, OH 45801
(419)222–9426

Canton Classic Car Museum
555 Market Avenue South
Canton, OH 44702
(216)455–3606

Carillon Historical Park
2001 S. Patterson Blvd.
Dayton, OH 45409
(513)293–2841

Charlie Sens Antique Auto Museum
2074 Marion Mt. Gilead Road
Marion, OH 43302–8991
(614)389–4686

Frederick C. Crawford Museum
10825 East Blvd.
Cleveland, OH 44106
(216)721–5722

Goodyear World of Rubber
1144 East Market Street
Akron, OH 44316
(216)796–7117

Portholes into the Past Museum
4450 Poe Road
Medina, OH 44256–5658
(216)725–0402

Toldeo Firefighters Museum
918 Sylvania Avenue
Toledo, OH 43613
(419)478–3473

Welsh Jaguar Classic Car Museum
5th and Washington Streets
P.O. Box 4130
Steubenville, OH 43952
(614)283–9723

OKLAHOMA

Mac's Antique Car Museum
1319 East 4th Street
Tulsa, OK 74120
(918)583–7400

Oklahoma State Firefighters Museum
2716 NE 50th Street
Oklahoma City, OK 73111
(405)424–3440

ONTARIO, CANADA

Canadian Automotive Museum
99 Simcoe Street South
Oshawa, ON L1H 4G7
(905)576–1222

OREGON

'77 Grand Prix Museum
16355 SE Yamhill
Portland, OR 97233
(503)252–5863

Tillamook County Pioneer Museum
2106 2nd Street
Tillamook, OR 97141
(503)842–4553

PENNSYLVANIA

Boyertown Museum of Historic Vehicles
29 Warwick Street
Boyertown, PA 19512–1415
(610)367–2090

Colonial Flying Corps Museum
Newark Road
Box 17
Toughkenamon, PA 19374
(610)268–2347

Corkins Automotive Restorations
233 East 3rd Street
Lewiston, PA 17044
(717)248–8181

Gast Classic Motorcars Exhibit
Route 896
421 Hartman Bridge Road
Strasburg, PA 17579
(717)687–9500

Harley-Davidson Museum
1425 Eden Road Museum
WTAMU Box 967
York, PA 17402
(717)848–1177 ext. 5900

JEM Classic Car Museum
Route 443, RD 1
Box 120C
Andreas, PA 18211
(717)386–3554

The State Museum of Pennsylvania
Third & North Streets
P.O. Box 1026
Harrisburg, PA 17120
(717)787–4978

Swigart Antique Auto Museum
28 Warwick Street
Huntingdon, PA 16652
(610)367–2090

RHODE ISLAND

Pronyne Motorsports Collectibles
114 Trenton Street
P.O. Box 1492
Pawtucket, RI 02862–1492
(401)725–1118

SOUTH CAROLINA

NMPA Stock Car Hall of Fame/Joe Weatherly Museum
Highway 34
P.O. Box 500
Darlington, SC 29532
(803)395–8821

SOUTH DAKOTA

Old West Museum
Highway I-90, Exit 260
P.O. Box 275
Chamberlain, SD 57325
(605)734–6157

Performance Car Museum
3505 S. Phillips Avenue
Sioux Falls, SD 57105
(605)338–4884

Pioneer Auto & Antique Town
Junction of I-90 & Highway 16 and 83
Murdon, SD 57559
(605)669–2691

TENNESSEE

Car Collectors Hall of Fame
1534 Demonbreun Street
Old Music Row
Nashville, TN 37203
(615)255–6804

Dixie Gun Works' Old Car Museum
Highway 51 South
One Gunpowder Lane
Union City, TN 38261
(901)885–0700

Smoky Mountain Car Museum
2970 Parkway
P.O. Box 1385
Pigeon Forge, TN 37868–1385
(615)453-3433

TEXAS

Alamo Classic Car Museum
6401 Interstate 35 South
New Braunfels, TX 78132
(210)606–4311

GAF Antique Auto Museum
118 Kodak Blvd.
P.O. Box 7189
Longview, TX 75607
(800)234–0124

Panhandle-Plains Historical Museum
US Highway 87 on 4th Avenue
Canyon, TX 79016

Pate Museum of Transportation
US Highway 377
P.O. Box 711
Fort Worth, TX 76101
(817)396–4305

UTAH

Classic Cars International Museum
355 West 700 South
Salt Lake City, UT 84101
(801)582–6883

Ogden Union Station Museum
Union Station
2501 Wall Avenue
Ogden, UT 84401
(801)629–8444

VERMONT

Bennington Museum
West Main Street
Bennington, VT 05201
(802)447–7166

VIRGINIA

Car and Carriage Caravan Museum
Carehill Road
P.O. Box 748
Luray Caverns Corp.
Luray, VA 22835
(703)743–6551 ext. 252

Glade Mountain Museum
Route 1
Box 360
Atkins, VA 24311
(540)783–5678

The Roaring Twenties Antique Car Museum
Route 1
Box 576
Hood, VA 22723
(703)948–6290

Rohr's Museum
9203 N. West
Box 71
Manassas, VA 22110
(703)368–3000

WASHINGTON

Lynden Pioneer Museum
217 W. Front Street
Lynden, WA 98264
(360)354–3675

WISCONSIN

Brooks Stevens Auto Museum
10325 N. Port Washington Road
Mequon, WI 53092
(414)241–4185

David Uihlein Antique Racing Car Museum
236 Hamilton Road
Turn Halle
Cedarburg, WI 53012
(414)253–2661

Hartford Heritage Auto Museum
147 N. Rural Street
Hartford, WI 53027
(414)673–7999

Zunker's Antique Car Museum
3722 MacArthur Drive
Manitowoc, WI 54220
(414)684–4005

Index

Ford Foundation, 83
Ford Hunger March, 78
Ford Motor Company, 30, 37, 39,
    41, 45, 46, 48, 49, 51, 52, 54, 55,
    58, 59, 60, 61, 63, 64, 67, 69, 71,
    74, 75, 76, 78, 80, 83, 85, 86, 89,
    91, 93, 94, 97, 98, 100, 101, 102,
    103, 104, 108, 110, 112, 113, 117,
    118, 121, 125, 126, 127, 129, 131,
    133, 135, 138, 142, 143, 144, 146,
    151, 158, 159, 161, 162, 163, 166,
    168, 169
Forecasts, 3, 5, 10, 16, 26, 27, 31, 37,
    56, 59, 60, 87, 90, 109, 155, 160,
    170
Four wheel drive, 28, 40, 89, 99, 107
Foyt, A. J., 142
France, 4, 7, 17, 24, 27, 28, 35, 37,
    40, 43, 51, 53, 58, 60, 64, 70, 81,
    84, 88, 93, 96, 116, 121, 130, 140,
    141, 151, 165, 169
France, Anatole, 37
Frank, Robert, 114
Frankfurt, Germany, 104
Franklin, 70
Franklin, Benjamin, 6
Frazer, 96, 105
Freeway shootings, 153, 159, 162
Freeways, 75, 87, 121, 127, 141, 157,
    160, 166
French Academy, 15
French Banque International, 35
Frey, Donald, 96
Front wheel drive, 25, 3, 81, 110,
    114, 117, 126, 134, 135, 144, 146.
Frost, George, 59
Fuel economy, 77, 84, 102, 100, 110,
    135, 136, 139, 140, 144, 156, 157,
    164
Fuel injection, 104
Fuji Heavy Industries, 110
Fuller, Buckminister, 79
Fulton, Robert, 8

Furnas, J. C., 81
Futurama, 87

Gabrielsson, Assar, 71
Gallatin, Albert, 10
Galleria Vittorio Emanuele, 14
Gandelot, Howard, 101
Garage door openers, 76
Garages, 25, 26, 31, 34, 44, 50, 70,
    76, 81, 84, 98, 106, 107
Garbage trucks, 46, 140
Garis, Howard, 35
Garlits, "Big Daddy," 135
Gas buggies, 28, 34, 35, 39
Gas gauge, 59
Gas pedal 31
Gas station pumps, 33
Gas stations. *See* Service stations
Gasoline, 14, 25, 27, 31, 34, 37, 42,
    44, 37, 42, 44, 55, 57, 61, 65, 71,
    73, 77, 80, 91, 93, 96, 102, 109,
    113, 118, 136, 141, 144, 164, 165
Gazette, The, 17
General Motors (G.M.), 39, 42, 50,
    51, 52, 54, 55, 57, 61, 63, 66, 67,
    70, 71, 77, 79, 82, 83, 84, 85, 89,
    90, 92, 93, 94, 95, 96, 97, 98, 100,
    101, 104, 105, 108, 110, 111, 112,
    113, 116, 120, 124, 127, 128, 129,
    130, 132, 133, 135, 138, 139, 142,
    145, 146, 147, 150, 151, 152, 153,
    155, 156, 158, 160, 162, 164, 166,
    168, 169, 170
General Tire, 50, 162
Gentlemen Highwaymen, 33
George Street, 14.
George Washington Bridge, 76, 167
Georgia, 40
German-Americans, 85
Germany, 5, 14, 16, 18, 30, 35, 42,
    45, 48, 49, 53, 56, 60, 63, 65, 70,
    72, 74, 75, 78, 80, 81, 84, 85, 86,
    87, 88, 89, 90, 91, 92, 93, 94, 96,

Museums, 55, 95, 103, 105, 118, 120,
    135, 143, 152, 154, 156, 160, 168,
    169, 170
Music, 26, 32, 46, 59, 66, 82, 83, 84,
    95, 98, 102, 105, 106, 107, 108,
    119, 124, 126, 140, 142, 145, 146,
    151, 169
Mussolini, Benito, 71, 74, 82
"My Merry Oldsmobile," 32
"My Mother the Car," 124

Nabokov, Vladimir, 108
Nader, Ralph, 108, 123, 135, 137, 143
Nahum, 2
Nantucket, 40
NASCAR, 98, 101
Nash, 51, 88, 90, 103, 108, 112
Nash, Charles W., 51
Nashville, 33, 66, 140
National Auto Chamber of Com-
    merce (Motor Vehicle Manufactur-
    ers' Association), 48, 51, 73, 75,
    169
National Defense and Interstate High-
    way Act, 110
National Highway Users Conference,
    77
National Industrial Recovery Act, 79
National Parks, 84, 142
National Road, 8, 9
National Safety Council, 49, 100, 107
National Transportation and Motor
    Safety Act, 125
Nazis, 61, 65, 80, 84, 85, 86, 90, 91,
    92, 97, 102
Nebraska, 158
Nelson, Gaylord, 131
A New England, 90
New Jersey, 12, 15, 17, 21, 32, 33,
    41, 57, 70, 71, 73, 91, 101, 136,
    152, 156, 157, 159, 167
New Jersey Turnpike, 101, 136, 157
New York Auto Show, 28, 32, 51

New York Central Railroad, 86
New York City, 4, 5, 6, 7, 9, 10, 11,
    13, 14, 22, 23, 24, 25, 26, 27, 28,
    29, 30, 31, 32, 33, 34, 36, 39, 44,
    45, 46, 47, 48, 49, 50, 51, 54, 59,
    61, 64, 65, 66, 69, 70, 73, 75, 76,
    77, 82, 84, 85, 86, 93, 101, 103,
    104, 105, 106, 107, 110, 112, 115,
    121, 123, 126, 127, 128, 129, 130,
    131, 132, 137, 138, 146, 153, 157,
    162
New York Herald, 34
New York State, 28, 29, 32, 40, 43,
    44, 46, 51, 55, 83, 85, 93, 115,
    125, 154, 158, 159
New York Stock Exchange, 9, 26, 43,
    72, 110
New York Times, 23, 31, 36, 47, 54,
    71
Newark, 46, 48, 77, 167
Newcomen, Thomas, 5
Newport, RI, 26
Newton, Isaac, 5
Nigeria, 111, 119, 136, 154
999 Monster, 31
Nineveh, 2
Nissan, 81, 84, 87, 105, 112, 113,
    126, 130, 140, 147, 151, 153, 156,
    157, 162, 164, 167
Nixon, Richard, 114, 132, 134, 136,
    139
Nobel Company, 15, 16
Nobility, 3, 6, 7, 10, 13, 21, 23, 28,
    30, 32, 36, 45, 48, 53, 56, 57, 61,
    78, 81, 106, 131, 134, 139, 140,
    150, 151
Nordoff, Heinz, 72
North America, 162, 165
Norton, Charles, 33
Norton, Edwin, 18
Novels, 11, 16, 30, 37, 40, 45, 53, 54,
    56, 58, 66, 70, 74, 80, 91, 94, 98,
    99, 100, 108, 111, 116, 117, 138

About the Author

CLAY McSHANE is Professor of History at Northeastern University and a noted authority on transportation history. Among his earlier publications is *Down the Asphalt Path: American Cities and the Automobile.*

ISBN 0-313-30308-8